DO THE NEXT
THING NEXT

Takes Your Landscaping Business to the Next
Level Even if You're Working 15 Hours
Every Day

BARRY RANDALL

INNER CIRCLE

Contents

I've worked with Barry for about 3 years but known him for 6. What really attracted me to working with Barry is how he spoke about business, which to me, gave me the clear confidence that he understood it all on a deeper level.

There are so many expert coaches out in the business world and I'm sure lots would help many business owners. But one that had specifically been in an almost identical industry AND been successful is indeed rare.

I very much believe in business you should only take advice from people who have been sat where you are and have been where you want to go.

In the time we have worked together my business has gone through massive change. I wanted to create a company that would be awesome to work for and was bigger than us all. To achieve that there is so much micro detail that needs to be done. This can be very much overwhelming. What Barry is great at, is improving areas of your business one step at a time.

At the start of working with Barry, we set a goal of achieving a £2m turnover. That has now been surpassed and we're aiming at £5m.

I've done lots of self-development and have studied business in my life. If you want to know how credible he is look at the first two sections of the book. 1st mindset. 2nd finances. Proof Barry knows exactly what he's talking about.

Barry is an inspiration to many and me. Plenty will be skeptical. But the truth is always the same, you can only lead a horse to water. It's up to you to take what he says and run with it.

Michael Wheat, Owner, Ponds by Michael Wheat

I started my business in 1997 as a landscape architect, and over the years, I've developed into a golf course designer.

In the early days, my business started by helping out one landscape architect in Rugby—who had some work on his books. Since then, I've been designing golf courses—for the last 20 odd years now.

I met Barry at a BNI event where he gave a small talk. At that exact moment, I switched on. I said, "Steve, there really is much more to business than just working in the business every day, doing golf course design, being on the sites with clients!" I realised how much I didn't know about things like marketing—which Barry did.

Here was someone who started where I did and now had a very, very good business himself. Not theoretical; this person really knew what they were talking about.

Barry has helped me realise I can't do everything by myself. I need some expertise in different areas: marketing, HR, recruitment, to name a few. There's so much more to all of it.

In a very short time Barry highlighted all of those areas where we really need to be concentrating if we want to build the business. Instead of going around and around, year after year, being very comfortable.

It's really only now that I've seen what can be done in a relatively short time. Just what Barry has done with his business. I can finally see the potential for growing my own business and you know... my biggest regret... is that I hadn't found this 20 years earlier!

Steve Ritson, Owner, Green Tyger Design

Having taken a leap to use Barry for his coaching services during what most people might have seen as a tough time economically, might have seemed foolish. I, however, knew enough of what Barry had achieved in his businesses and the businesses of others to know that making the decision to take Barry on balanced well in my favour.

Working with Barry has helped me to direct the scatty entrepreneurial side of my brain to focus on the important issues facing me, whilst not forgetting about the longer term ambitions and putting the right tasks and jobs first, which will then set me on the right path for those bigger more audacious dreams to be actioned when appropriate.

Barry has an approach that others in his field may not —he's owned a business, grown a business, made the mistakes and learnt from them, so can educate and teach from a good position himself. His advice and thoughts come from experience, this means we don't make the same mistakes or can be quicker to make the crucial calls. Because he has given us the tools to look ahead and forecast growth, bottlenecks, and change.

Barry is a great guy, real in character and experience, no fake façade, and keen to see you and your business thrive in whatever market you are in!

Matthew Ward, Owner, True Roots Carpentry & Joinery

I started my business for family reasons and to give myself the opportunity to earn more money. Like everyone else, business started off really exciting and fairly easy. I was working away not realising the business was starting to run me instead of me running it. The usual problems arose; no time for myself... inconsistent work schedules... problems with employees. Then as the business became more scrambled, a lot more unorganised.

I met Barry and he introduced me to his early 12-week course. I was unsure at first, but after joining I quickly gained clarity about what was wrong with the business. I quickly established a vision for the business. I knew that was a skill that Barry possessed. I just didn't realise it was so easily transferable to me.

Being part of the program, I learnt new systems to put in place, whether it be hiring new employees, higher pricing structures, using time-saving qualifications. Just all these things that seemed insignificant previously, are now integral parts of the day to day running of the business.

Before I did the course running the business was hard work. I was getting up early in the morning, getting in the van and hoping for the best basically. I had to do all the physical work and the business owner work, because I was relying on people that weren't necessarily skilled enough to do the work with me. It was a constant repetitive cycle of tying myself in knots.

There was no real logistical planning in place for the day to day work, whether that's being on-site or the administrative side of things... It was just way more difficult to manage.

I was wondering about joining the club for a while, and with hindsight, it was just a case of taking the plunge and going for it. Because at the end of the day, running a business was so confusing, but it doesn't have to be, if you've got the right support there for you. Support that makes it simple and provides you with clarity. Which is what the club does. I realise now all that was holding me back from making my business easier to run was a small monthly investment and me being brave enough to take that step... because it made everything easier for me.

Tom Scharenheuvel Lewitt, Owner, Clearspace Groundcare

Owning responsibility of a business and embracing entrepreneurship takes pure grit and consistent persistence! It can also be a lonely minefield of uncertainties from time to time. Feeling depleted in my game, I decided to travel from overseas to attended Barry's two-day business re-vamp in the UK. And I'm so very grateful I did.

Barry offered refreshingly straightforward and actionable advice. He has all the tools, templates, and tried and tested methods, that have given me proven results. He openly shares and mentors with an abundance mindset, and he genuinely wants all in his groups to succeed. I also had the pleasure to meet with a wonderful mix of like-minded peers (now good friends).

Moving forward, we all regularly help each other in business and genuine friendships alike. Whether you're just starting out or a seasoned veteran of your game, I would highly recommend to connect with Barry. You won't have time to look back as you power energetically forward.

Andy Keane, Greenacres Landscapes

It has been life changing. I can highly recommend Barry to anyone else looking to transform their business overnight.

His down to earth approach is what attracted us to him when we first spoke. He didn't try and talk us into anything but offered me great advice. Since working with him we have grown the business in areas we wouldn't have known how to.

Not only does he have the tools and systems, he offers around the clock support - nothing is too much trouble for him. A genuinely nice, helpful and knowledgeable guy.

Benedict Bonsor, Director, Orbro-Reed Landscapes

I have been running my landscaping business for 18 years. From the day I set the business up, I was always ambitious. I wanted to be the biggest and best business in Harrogate. But whatever I did I seemed to be in a rut, which I could never seem to get out of.

I successfully completed a large number of big jobs. I won numerous 'best in shows' for our show gardens. I even had a beautiful website... and various other things that I thought would take my business to the next level.

I had spoken to various business coaches, but none of them seemed to get the problems I was having. None of them had been up to their knees in mud, knowing you would still make a loss on the job, or taken on a landscaping job at a low price, just because you were desperate for work!

Four years ago, it got to a real turning point in my life. I was going through a divorce. I was up to my eyes in debt. To cap it all I'd had to pull out of a dream trip to New Zealand to see the British Lions because the business couldn't work without me around.

I knew things needed to change. Just as I did, I saw Barry speak at an event in Leeds, and I knew straight away this was a guy I wanted to work with. In fact, the story he was telling was so similar to mine it was scary.

I went to a couple of Barry's one-day workshops, and then in January 2020 I bit the bullet and joined his Landscaper's Success Club Black Diamond group. Finally, I had someone who understood my problems. Someone who had been in the same trenches as me.

Using Barry's teachings has rapidly grown my business, in what could have been a very difficult year. Commercially I have more than doubled the size of my business—in less than a year! That's turnover AND profit. To cap it all, I have just booked my dream trip to see the British Lions tour South Africa in 2021, which I mark as a real benchmark of success.

For anyone in the landscaping industry who wants to change their business, I would highly recommend working with him. Join his Black Diamond group. Consume his content. Open your mind and listen.

Barry is changing people's lives, and he's a genuine guy who I'm now proud to call my friend.

David Massey, Owner, David Massey Garden Construction

I originally stumbled across the name Barry Randall via LinkedIn and essentially I just clicked follow. It was that simple. The problems I was facing at the time resonated with almost everything you posted. I began to pay a bit more attention. Then a little bit more. Before I took action and we started chatting.

Meeting you virtually six months ago has proven to be the best and most important decision of my business life so far. Not only do you have the knowledge and skills that I need, but you deliver in such a way it would be rude to not essentially do as I'm told—and this is what I've done.

You are a genuine, honest, and kind human being that I'm privileged to know, to even have your personal phone number in my phone is an honour. I messaged you a few weeks ago thanking you for turning me into a better father! I did not expect that. It didn't even come into my thinking when I joined this group!

Because of YOU in order of importance I'm a far better father, a far better husband, a much more rounded businessman. And really just a better, more rounded person. Thank you for everything and seriously this platform is too small to truly show how grateful I am for what you have given me, Claire and our children.

The above is my love letter to you mate! You mean the world to me and I wish you and your inspiring family all the success in the world. You deserve it.

Daren Henderson, Owner, Edinburgh Driveway Company

Very honored to have Barry as a longtime member of our elite business mastermind. Because he's both been in the trenches as a top tradesman, and is now coaching others in that field, he brings a unique and super-valuable real-world insight to solving the problems of successful marketing.

We even have something called the 'Barry Quotient" now: It's a scale on following through and implementing the ideas you receive in the group. Even veteran marketers can't touch Barry's dedication to road-testing concepts and tactics to guarantee they work. His followers are damned lucky to have him as their field general.

John Carlton, the most ripped-off and respected copywriter alive

---

Barry is the rare person who has built a successful business over decades and is still committed to learning and applying marketing strategies and techniques that work TODAY.

The growing list of business owners Barry is helping increase sales and, at the same time, get their business and lives under control is proof that what he will teach you is both effective and realistic.

Stan Dahl, CEO, Marketing Rebel LLC

Just for anyone who is thinking of using Barry for future 1-2-1 sessions, here is a bit (understatement) about how he has enhanced our company, given us hope, increased sales/profitability, and encouraged confidence we never knew we had. We had lost that 'fire in our belly', the drive and sight of our goals. We were 'plodders', same shit different day. Our relationship was suffering, we were tired, frustrated, and uninspired.

In September 2019 Chris and I had decided that we needed help. The business was stagnant, we weren't profiting any money, we had two very destructive and draining team members where we weren't even the bosses in our own business, savings were getting lower and lower of Chris's personal money—we had reached a point where the love for being self-employed was diminished. Sleepless night after night worrying about finances, abusive and controlling team members, where the next job is going to come from etc., etc… the list goes on as I am sure it does for most of you.

We contacted Barry after being recommended, unsure of what to expect or how it was all going to pan out we were, like anyone would be, apprehensive. Our initial consultation went well (even though he didn't offer to buy us a coffee)—we were completely transparent with our goals, financial situation, and our flaws. Barry reassured us that we have great foundations to make it into something brilliant, we signed the agreement (still parched at this point I might add) and left to come home feeling hopeful and refreshed.

In the six months we had 1-2-1 coaching and also attending a couple of his group events it has transformed our business! Soooo much has changed to the point our business is unrecognisable. We cut the dead wood out and began afresh with some new team members and embraced the good crew we already had! We have doubled our prices; we are confident in our pricing and profits have massively increased! Oakham Garden Services now has funds in the bank to reinvest on tools, courses, vans, our employees etc!

We recently have agreed a LET on an office space,

allowing clients to come in and visit us to see products and discuss proposals. Also now have a space for team meetings and group training, the lads have somewhere to pop in to for a cuppa and a catch up at the end of the week—this has been a HUGE weight off my shoulders, meaning I could get my dining room back and finally rid of all the paperwork!

Things are run more proficiently and professionally, everything is in order, filed and put away. Needless to say, that we share the office building with our accountant, and we aren't able to use the space until this pandemic calms down, so for now my dining room has come to the rescue, again!!!

Overall, if you are thinking about having coaching, you need to STOP and just do it but also embrace it and enjoy the journey! It has changed our lives, it's changed our employees' lives and the clients we provide a service to.

For every moment you're thinking about having coaching is another minute wasted—don't waste time pondering over something that is going to enrich your life, double your money and will benefit you, your family and workers! You went self-employed for a reason, the same reason as everyone else, you have the opportunity to pay for knowledge where someone has made all the same mistakes you have and are going to.

And Barry, thank you so much for everything you have done. Chris and I are truly grateful. It may sound over the top to anyone who hasn't already had coaching, but you have changed our lives. You should write a book, could be a great seller ;-)

Benn Parkinson, Owner, Oakham Garden Services

I've been fortunate to spend decades working with and around high achievers who seem to possess superhuman abilities to identify and accomplish big goals. Barry, however, is in a class by himself. He is the rare individual who focuses his attention like a laser on what matters most, then works relentlessly to get it done day in and day out.

More importantly, he is able to teach others how to do the same. This book is a collection of Barry's wisdom - buy it, read it, take action, and then watch what happens when your life changes for the better.

Shawn Twing, Founder, Barn Door Media, LLC

If you're aiming to reach the top of the game in your industry, gaining access to proven tools for success, continual growth and maximized profits are imperative.

Barry openly shares his systems, processes, stories, secrets and hard-core business tactics in his latest book. I'd recommend this tool as the quickest way to reach your goals and end on an extremely high note!

Lori Haller, Designing Response, LLC

I've known Barry for a few years now and watched in awe as he quickly created a brand new, additional business from the ground up with astonishing speed.

His positive, rapid-implementation approach to business has been an inspiration to me. If you have a chance to learn from him, I suggest you don't hesitate to do so.

David Deutsch, A-List Copywriter

For ten years my business was growing and shrinking on a regular and repeating cycle. I had nothing in place to control and manage the growth, which meant I always ended up back at square one.

I've never had a solid plan to get to where I wanted to be. I knew what I wanted but was lacking the belief to achieve it. What I wanted was more me time, which never happened. That added to the frustration, stress and ever-growing costs.

It wasn't until I read Barry's first book (*Time, Team & Money*) that I finally understood; without the right knowledge and help from someone who knew what I wanted to achieve. Without the exact methods of how to do it—I would carry on repeating my previous mistakes and struggle to grow a successful business.

I can now see the path forward. I have a plan and a vision of where I want to be. I have a clarity for the first time in ten years.

James Braid, Owner, MCS Landscaping Ltd

I had been running a garden and landscaping business for over a decade. I loved. But it was all-consuming and failing in so many typical areas; profitability, staff issues, expansion failures and never enough time.

Repeating the same mistakes and frustrations year on year and never finding a solution; no time to address the issues as always needing to finish the next quote, design, and project to keep the cash flowing to pay the bills.

I stumbled across an advert for a course Barry was advertising called 'double your digits'. Initially 1 was sceptical, wondered if it was a scam but took a risk and signed up. The course covered the content of his first book. It was insightful advice how a struggling business owner, who I identified with, turned his landscaping company into a successful business.

This started my journey with Barry... attending further courses, membership programs and opening more opportunities for my business and myself.

18 months later 1 am reading Barry's second book, reflecting on how far the business has come.

His guidance has led to the following successes:

- Myself coming off the tools to concentrate on design, quotes, and working on the business - giving me more personal time.
- The landscaping teams expanded with good staff following the *Time, Team and Money* recruitment process.
- Charging for Garden Design Services that 1 used to do for free, which has increased my income.
- Improved marketing to attract clients at increased prices and still winning more work.
- Additional support staff to reduce workload on myself but who can actually do a better job than myself.
- Putting processes in place to monitor

performance of the teams, business and marketing.

- Additional product offerings to clients to aid retention and provide new business opportunities.

There's still a lot more to do but I feel so positive about the future and creating the business l dream of because of Barry's support.

Craig McGibbon, Owner, Craig McGibbon Garden Design

————————————

We turned to Barry for help because we felt 'stuck' in our business and had found ourselves working endless hours - in the false belief we needed to work harder for it to get better. But 15 years in, we still had the same business.

In less than a year, Barry has helped us to introduce everything we were missing in our business.

He gave us passion for our marketing and showed us ways to stand out and be different.

He helped us create a recruitment process that works! Which helped us build a team who are invested in our business and its growth.

His mentoring style is personable, he's always available, and his knowledge and ability to explain things which seem confusing in a simple to understand way is awesome.

With Barry's guidance, both myself and Rich have grown as business owners and also as people. We have more confidence, more courage, and more capabilities.

His advice and guidance are always exactly what we need when we need it.

Having someone to help you see clearly when you come up against a problem you've never faced before is priceless.

Barry has changed our lives.

Kate O'Gleby-Smith, Owner, BASH Grab & Skip Hire

––––––––––––––––

My company was producing some great quality work, but it was consuming all of my time and I was struggling to make a steady profit on many of my projects.

Much of each day was spent firefighting behind the scenes, and in truth I was exhausted.

Since working with Barry my turnover has increased, my profit margins are up, my clients are happier, and everything is calmer. I know that all sounds too good to be true, and there have been some bumps along the way.

But when I look back, I can't believe the progress I've made. I am now excited about the future of my business and very aware of how much more I can achieve.

In short, I have got my life back. Barry helped me to focus on the areas that needed improving straight away, set me deadlines (who doesn't need a deadline!) and he is still helping me to make huge improvements.

There's been lots of practical advice as well as a bit of blue-sky thinking. Oh—and I'm having a lot of fun too.

Barry has helped me to rediscover the joy of running my own business.

Brett Hardy, Owner, Brett Hardy Landscapes

From the age of 16 I knew landscaping was my passion!

I went and studied Horticulture at Bishop Burton College. I then went to further extend my knowledge at Leeds University to study Landscape Architecture that led me to go to Australia and worked on high-end Garden Design projects for three years. Why am I telling you all this? Simple!

After all of my eight years learning and studying the art of landscaping, I can honestly say, within the six months of knowing Barry, I have truly learnt the art of landscaping and what it genuinely takes to become successful within the industry!

At the age of now 27, I have just bought my first home for £265,000, I am completely debt-free and can now be in a position to sit down and write down goals I want to achieve, which would only've ever been a dream in the back of my mind!

Landscaping is much more than laying patios and building walls, and now that Barry's opened my eyes to all the endless possibilities, I'm never going to close them again!

John Tallis, Operations Manager, David Massey Garden Construction

WARNING! Do not listen to Barry Randall unless… you're prepared to take your business from a rough gem and turn it into a flawless diamond!

Barry has the uncanny ability to turn an ordinary businesses into beyond extraordinary… by delivering such a potent cocktail of business success… **ANY** savvy business owner would be lining up at the bar to drink it.

Not only does he walk the talk… he's got a huge heart and he genuinely cares about people's success.

As my business partner, I couldn't ask for anyone more ethical or committed.

When you want to create unlimited success in your life, be wise and talk with Barry. You'll be very glad you did.

Trevor 'ToeCracker' Crook, **Business Mentor**

We wanted to expand from a small business to a larger, more profitable one, but didn't really have a plan of how to do it. We had grown our turnover but weren't seeing the reward for our extra efforts.

Before our first meeting with Barry, we were a bit sceptical of his claims and were expecting the sales banter; almost like the window salesman coming around. But he was straight to the point and got down to the bare bones of the business very quickly. In just one hour he identified issues that should have been so obvious, yet somehow aren't when you're so immersed, (buried), in the day-to-day running of the business. And why were we so buried in it all? Well, that is exactly what he made clear in the second hour of that first meeting!

It didn't take long for us to see the plan for our business should be so different to what it actually was. Barry made us realise we could get so much more out of life with less effort if we worked smarter.

After a session with Barry you will understand:

1. A completely new way of looking at your

business and how it should be run.

2. The path you will need to follow.

3. He will help you along that path and aid you with all the decisions that need to be made and when.

4. That you have the power to develop your business into a great business that earns you more money and freedom.

Put simply, Barry cuts away the unnecessary, provides you with pure clarity, teaches the way forward with support, and infuses it all with an infectious positivity and enthusiasm.

There will be a few tough moments, but that is all part of the learning curve and you feel better and stronger as you conquer each one. The good thing is: we always feel like we're moving towards our end goal, which helps spur you on. We very much look forward to the future and hope to maintain a strong relationship along the way.

Thank you Barry!

Travers Bryan, Owner, AJ Bryan Construction

————————————

If there is one person's advice that you can trust to significantly increase your business while reducing your time spent in the business, it's Barry.

When this man speaks, the ONLY thing you need to do is listen, implement and enjoy the inevitable profit that's coming your way.

Stephen Somers, Co-Founder, Marketplace Superheroes

This book is dedicated to my late mother-in-law, Stephanie Yvonne Smith, who showed me what someone with a positive mindset really looks like.
For that, I'll be forever grateful.

Foreword

Wayne Grills, CEO, British Association of
Landscape Industries (BALI)

I was thrilled to be asked by Barry to write the foreword for his latest book. My name is Wayne Grills, and Barry and I first met several years ago when his company, the Leicestershire Garden Design Company became a BALI member. Barry has kept in touch and it's been pleasing to see his business grow and improve over the years.

During one of my many member visits with Barry, we discussed how he was changing his business and his desire to help and support others in the industry, to help them emulate the success he's seen with his own business. He has a passion and a desire to support small-to-medium-sized businesses and to effect change for those who want to change how they run their businesses.

Often, the changes required go beyond the business—and in reading this book, you'll see that Barry provides a range of practical advice and tips based on real-life experiences, on how to take those steps and make changes to your business, including many testimonials from those who have read his books, attended his success clubs, and benefitted from his ongoing support.

This book is all about asking yourself the right questions and taking steps to effect change. He talks about making choices for you and your business, and provides practical solutions on how to overcome your fear barriers and instil confidence in the decisions you take. He talks about how to look after others involved in your business, like staff, clients, and suppliers.

So, now is the time to read on and immerse yourself in the book and ensure that you take time to progress yourself in order to progress your business.

In other words, work *on it*, not in it—just as Barry has done. Give it a try. If you don't make changes, you'll be doing the same thing again next week!

Wayne Grills

———————————

Wayne is the Chief Executive of the British Association of Landscape Industries (BALI)—the UK's leading Trade Association for landscape contractors/gardeners, garden designers and suppliers to the landscape industry. BALI has over 940 registered members, employing over 102,000 staff, and has a combined annual turnover of over £12 billion.

PREFACE

Never Take Business Advice from Someone Who Hasn't Been Where You Are Now

Let me give you the context before I give you all the content.

It all started with a fairly typical, all-too-familiar kick in the teeth (metaphorically speaking).

I'll never forget the meeting. It was the afternoon of Friday, October 12, 2012, at the Citizens Advice Bureau in Loughborough, Leicestershire.

It was an unusually warm autumn afternoon—the perfect weather for finishing off a garden design, which is what I was doing the morning of the meeting. In typical Barry fashion, I was cutting it fine with the time, and my wife was getting anxious.

Rushing home, I jumped in the shower. Part of me was excited about the meeting at the CAB, but part of me was terrified of finding out just how bad things were. I'd backed myself into a corner, working 15-hour days, often seven days a week, simply to pay for the basics like keeping a roof over our heads and the kids clothed.

If I didn't work the 15-hour days, we constantly had money problems and customers complaining and pestering me. If I did work the 15-hour days, my personal life suffered. My relationship with Marie, my wife, was strained, to say the least. I was at my lowest point ever and wanted desperately to find the answers, so I could look my wife and children in the eyes and say, "I did it." Like any father, I wanted to make them proud.

The journey to the Citizens Advice Bureau was silent. I had a sick feeling in the pit of my stomach. The ride back was even quieter, but inside my head, there was a festival going on. On the way there, I thought things were probably pretty grim, but I didn't know for sure. On the way home, I KNEW how bad everything really was.

I spent ages circling the car park. I wasn't putting off the moment of truth; I was looking for a wide space. Marie told me, "Just park there!" at least three times, but I kept circling. I used the excuse of needing enough room to back out safely, but the truth was I wanted to make sure nobody would damage my car door when they parked next to me.

Secretly, I knew I couldn't afford the few pounds it would cost to get a scratch removed. It was just one more thing from which I was 'protecting' my family. I couldn't admit to them, "If the door gets damaged, we'll have to leave it like that because we don't have the cash to pay for it." I knew it would worry them, and it's my job to protect them, not cause them concern.

The car parking thing still exists today. I don't think I'll ever get over people banging their car door against mine, although the disagreements are funnier these days. We can laugh about it now.

Inside the Citizens Advice Bureau

The Citizens Advice Bureau was old, dated, and felt more like an accountant's office. It had the usual warning signs: report this, report that; not very warm and welcoming. It was exactly the kind of place you would expect to go when you had a problem.

We waited in silence for what seemed like hours until, eventually, a very happy-go-lucky lady came down the corridor.

"Barry and Marie?" she said.

Her relaxed, laid-back nature struck me immediately. She was middle-aged, well-presented, with a great big smile. She was chatty and put us both at ease immediately. I remember envying her lack of stress and the freedom she obviously felt.

Inside the room, we got talking about the problem I was having with my business and personal finances. How the first cracks appeared after the 2008 recession—and how things had slowly declined.

"How bad is it?" she asked.

I looked my wife in the eyes, and for the first time, I was able to get the words out.

"I'm five months behind on my mortgage."

Just as calm and relaxed as before, the lady asked, "Have you had any advice from a debt management specialist?"

"Yes, but it's made matters worse," I said. "I'm five months behind on my second mortgage, too, and my parents live at that house."

I stared at Marie, and the full weight of the position I had put my family in hit me. We were vulnerable and on the brink of losing everything. My fear of failure was crushing me.

I wanted to blame the debt management advice I'd had, but it was advice I could have refused. I wanted to blame the recession, but the recession happened four years ago.

The truth was, I had a bad relationship with money.

I asked what my options were, and the CAB lady said, "Pay the arrears, or you'll lose the house."

I was devastated—but somehow, I also felt free. Because I was out of choices, and something had to change. The same thinking that got me into this position was not going to get me out of it.

If I wanted things to change, I had to change.

Having clarity for the first time about my finances and my lack of options made me more excited. I didn't have to keep getting up every day, jumping into my van and pretending my troubles didn't exist. Living a life of pretence is exhausting, and I was now free to work on the problem.

A client had given me a book a few months before the meeting at the CAB, but I'd never read it. I didn't read books as a rule, but that meeting at the CAB made me read the one my client had given me. It gave me the courage to meet my coach for the first time. It gave me back the energy I had lost, trying to fight all the problems in my business.

I felt like I did on the first day I opened my business: the same excitement about heading into the unknown, which I had lost one knock at a time. It was energising. I'd always wanted to go back and start my business again with the knowledge I'd gained and with someone who could answer my questions before I suffered from my lack of knowledge.

Here was my chance.

I felt lucky then—and I want you to feel lucky too. When you've finished reading this book, I believe you'll have the same energy and excitement you had on day one of your business. I'm so confident I can keep that promise that if you don't feel it, you can write and let me know and I'll send you a full refund for your book.

As you read on, I want you to hold on to this mindset: it's never too late to change and turn it all around.

INTRODUCTION

Good at Landscaping, Poor at Business

"Pay the arrears, or you'll lose the house."

Those words echoed in my head.

I was £90,000 in debt, working 15-hour days, and I had no idea how to get off the hamster wheel. I lurched from one disaster to another. I was sinking financially and trying to figure out answers to questions I'd never faced before. I had nowhere to turn for help.

My relationship with my wife and daughters was non-existent. I'm ashamed to say I had no time for anyone or anything. The people I was supposed to be doing this for were getting nothing. At the time, it felt like I was trying to make it work; but in reality, I was making life worse.

When I did force some time off, I was always distracted by the problems lurking in the background—dashing off to the toilet to check emails or 'quickly' answering a call. I felt I could relax more when I knew what was going on, but that's a poor excuse and just made me feel worse.

I'd snap at the most stupid things. Problems and frustrations I hadn't dealt with at work would turn into shouting at the kids or petty squabbles with my wife. I gave ungrateful customers and selfish employees all my time and attention and wasn't there for the people who cared most about me.

Not because I didn't want to—I yearned to give my

time to them! I wanted to have good things and good times, but my workload just consumed every waking minute.

I didn't have enough time to get the work done, never mind putting effort into family time or friendships. The business had its claws into me, and I felt trapped by work, recurring bills, and mounting debts.

It was *always* 15-hour days, *always*—and most of it on underpriced work just so I could keep my head above water. I took on jobs solely to pay wages or have cashflow. I ignored customer complaints because I couldn't afford to deal with them properly. I was continually looking over my shoulder and dreading the phone ringing.

I was so stressed I eventually collapsed in my bathroom one evening while brushing my teeth. I fell backwards, banged my head on the radiator, and bit my tongue. I came around, and my tongue was bleeding.

Marie, my wife, was puzzled. "What are you doing?" she asked.

I didn't know what had happened.

That incident scared me enough to see the doctor, and I don't go to the doctor unless I'm seriously ill. He said it sounded like I had fainted. After some tests and a couple of weeks waiting for the results, I found out I had a dangerously high cholesterol level, brought on by stress, overwork, and poor diet.

As any good doctor does, he told me to take some time off and rest. Ha! That instruction just reminded me why I didn't go to the doctors. If you go to the doctors, they'll tell you to rest.

Something I could not possibly do.

The remedy is simple; the reality is anything but. As you know, when you run a business, it's not as easy as taking time off and relaxing. I had to keep going. I had bills to pay and customers to pacify.

My hamster wheel kept spinning: The next job needs selling, this project needs organising, little Jonny has called in sick, another customer complaint, chasing payments because the merchants had put me on stop with my accounts. You name it—I had to deal with it.

But it was about to get a whole lot worse, and the scariest thing was I couldn't see it coming because I was so busy trying to keep the business going. I had never felt more helpless and powerless in my life.

When I discovered how bad things really were during the CAB meeting, it was like an arrow through my heart. Everything I'd put into this business, all my blood, sweat, and tears, had brought me to the point of collapse.

I was devastated. I was embarrassed. I was shocked.

But here's the thing; I also got the clarity and courage to face up to my problems for the first time.

Lots of things were going wrong for me, and I was getting further and further behind—but I wasn't alone.

I thought I was.

I wasn't.

I never was.

I just didn't realise the same thing was happening all around me, every day.

I was amazed. Every business owner I've ever talked with has suffered from this exact problem at one time or another. Many continue to struggle and never get free of their hamster wheels—like Alan Kingsberry, from Belfast:

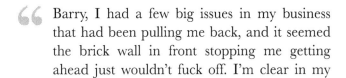

Barry, I had a few big issues in my business that had been pulling me back, and it seemed the brick wall in front stopping me getting ahead just wouldn't fuck off. I'm clear in my mind now how to solve those problems and push on. That's down to getting your sound advice, and I'll be forever grateful for that help.

We don't have to do this alone. I'm profoundly grateful I found the answers when I did.

I don't want you to suffer the same fate, which is why I'm putting my story on paper and reaching out to people just like you.

What I'm going to share with you in each chapter of this book changed EVERYTHING for me. I felt helpless, powerless, and drained of energy.

Then, in a single moment of clarity, I felt free—and all my energy returned, leaving me feeling as if it was the first day of my new business. It was like an imaginary line drawn in the sand.

I had a mountain of problems:

- No time
- Poor-paying customers
- Ungrateful employees
- Debt
- Nowhere to turn for support
- Too much responsibility
- People who didn't understand my problems

Even the weather was unkind to me.

But in one sentence, I got the truth I had needed for a long time. It shook me to the soles of my steel toe-cap boots. It gave me perspective and a chance, which was all I wanted—a chance to start again with a clean slate. And here it was in the most simplistic way possible.

I only had ONE problem.

It was staring me in the face every morning, and I couldn't see it.

I was trapped. I didn't know what I was doing. I had no definite way to fix it. Realistically, I was never going to find the answers on my own. Which is why I think you and I have a lot in common.

Looking back, I was waiting for someone to come along and save me. Then I heard eight words that sank deep into my heart and tripped a switch.

"For things to change, first YOU must change."

OMG (as my daughter would say).

How simple is this concept? I didn't need to change everything; I just needed to change one thing.

We can't change the mountain of problems. The lack of time. Poor-paying customers. Ungrateful employees. The unpaid debt. The lack of professional support. Taking on too much responsibility. Having people around who don't understand your problems. Certainly, we can't change the awful weather.

We can't change any of it unless we change ourselves.

Instead of killing myself trying to fix it all on my own, I could take advice from someone who knew the answers. My job was to find the person who could help me improve things, not do the fixing myself. I didn't need to have all the answers—it was my job as the business owner to find someone who did.

If I changed my thinking and saw recruiting people who are more skilled than me as a sign of intelligence, rather than weakness, I could win. I didn't need to struggle along trying to build a business by trial and error when there were people out there who already knew how to do it.

With that new mindset, I started to read as much information, take on as many mentors, and learn from as many experts as I could. I started making changes. I took massive actions one small step at a time, focusing only on doing the next thing next. The biggest challenge was not doing too much at once because day by day, quicker than I expected, I started to get my life back.

Over the past eight years, I've grown a multi-million-pound landscaping business and helped hundreds of people just like you transform their businesses using the same systems, the same processes, and the same mindset. I'm not a preacher of business methods; I'm a rolled-up-sleeves, in-the-trenches business owner, experiencing the same problems as you, day in, day out.

Is it easy? No, of course it isn't. If it were, you'd already be doing it, and I wouldn't need to write this introduction and lay it out in front of you.

Throughout every chapter of this book, I present you with some solid business (and life) skills and advice. I share real-life stories, testimonials, and guidance from some of the business owners I've had the pleasure of working with along my journey.

I pass on some of the best quotes and ideas people have shared as well and explain what they mean to me. I dive deep into the emotional parts of my personal journey, and you'll discover why I believe anyone can go from struggling to thriving with the right systems and mindset. I also make a single promise that I'll help you find the courage to take these first steps for your own business.

Believe me, I'm not writing this book with rose-tinted glasses on. When you see how many times I've messed up myself (and some of them quite spectacularly), you'll see it's not genius thinking that takes you from struggling to thriving; it's a strong mindset, a positive work ethic, and having great people around you.

And sometimes you need a good dressing down and

someone to give it to you straight, which is what I'm about to do.

So enjoy all of it.

A client of mine, Michael, said to me once, "When my business is struggling I need to be told I've got it wrong, not have a cheerleader telling me everything's going to be ok, and that's what I like about you."

If you like real-life examples, love learning from other people's struggles, want to simplify your problems, and you're willing to do the work, I want to make you this promise:

This book will give you back your life.

It's full of practical advice you can implement to make considerable changes to your life and business—and it will also help you to:

- Remove the fixed mindset that's controlling you and keeping you trapped
- Get you straight about money and what's rightfully yours
- Acquire the skills to find and attract high-end customers
- Understand all the systems you need to make business simple
- Truly believe you can transform your personal life

There's only one thing that might stand in the way.
You.
I need to know you're ready to change.
Being a victim of your circumstances isn't an excuse anymore. It's taking away ALL the power you possess to

design and build a wonderful life for you, your loved ones, and the people you employ.

I want you to believe me when I say, YOU have the power to make significant changes right now.

But you also have to believe that only you can make those changes.

Only you can say, "I've had enough of the old way. I'm ready to do things differently."

If you're not willing to change, I'll stop you now.

You should put this book down.

My Dad always said, "There's no such thing as can't. Take the 'T' off, and what have you got?"

You CAN do it if you're ready.

This decision should be a simple one for you to make because in the end there are only two options. You either *won't* change your business, and things continue as they are now. Or you *want* to change—and you're ready to take the first step.

These are your choices.

Every successful person has a story about change. Every successful person has a moment it all came together, and this is yours. So, let's dive deep.

If you're ready to change right now, put the book down for a moment. Email me and tell me exactly what you want to change in your business and what you want your life to be like.

Write to me at barry@barryrandall.co.uk with the subject line: 'I'm ready to change.' Make a note of the date, so it sticks in your mind forever.

Just like mine… **Friday, October 12, 2012.**

Then pick the book up again and read on.

1

MINDSET IS EVERYTHING

Success Happens Inside Your Head First

> *You can't go back and change the beginning, but you can start where you are and change the ending.*
> **C.S. Lewis**

The first book I read with any intent to learn was a book called *The E-Myth* by Michael Gerber. Before then, I read to my daughters, and before that, to my little brother as part of his primary school education (I seem to remember one book especially well called *Roger Red Hat*. No idea why I still remember that book!).

Interestingly, the only book I had read myself was half of an autobiography by one of my favourite boxers, the Welsh Hall of Famer, Joe Calzaghe. I fondly remember my stop/start go at reading it about a year or so before when we were on holiday in Spain. I made a very lame attempt to relax while I was away. But, as always, I was easily side-tracked by the free-flowing, ever-present, all-inclusive bar at the hotel. Who isn't?

The E-Myth was the first book I read that made me stop and think. **"You don't know what you don't know"** is one of those awesome, penny-dropping moment quotes I came across in the early part of my personal development journey.

In my previous book, *Time, Team and Money: How to create more time, build a better team, and make more money without going round in circles* I talked in-depth about *The E-Myth* and how one person's insistence I read the book helped me overcome my fear of the unknown. I'll recap briefly here.

Richard was a client of mine who almost wasn't. I'd arrived back from a trip, and the client we were supposed to be working for had cancelled the project on us. At the time, I blamed the client, but the truth was I never had a Plan B. Anyway, I called Richard and asked if he still wanted the garden building. To my surprise, he said yes, and was ready to start immediately if I could get the price right. To cut a long story short, we agreed on the fee and the work started the very next week.

During the build, Richard pulled me to one side and said, "You have people working for you on-site, yet you're doing all of the physical labour, working with me on the quoting and planning, and going off to quote for future work. Do you not have a system to make that easier?"

I must have looked at him like he had two heads, because he immediately said, "Do you read books?"

"I once read half of Joe Calzaghe's autobiography," I said, jokingly.

My default reaction to being unsure was to make a joke of the situation. A good witty joke often helped me through not knowing how to answer a question correctly. Richard said, "I mean business books on mindset." He went inside and brought out a book wrapped in celebration paper. He gave it to me and said, "Read this book; it'll change everything for you."

What I didn't realise at the time was that Richard's gesture was part of a referral scheme from his business coach. Of course, he was a nice guy and wanted to offer me some help—that's what being in the self-development bubble does for you. It's why I'm writing this now. When I got in the van and out of Richard's sight, I tore off the paper to see what was inside.

It was a copy of *The E-Myth*.

I threw the book on the dashboard of my van with the rest of the receipts, newspapers, and such like, which had started to accumulate like bad memories. For the next few weeks, Richard repeatedly asked me if I had read the book, and every time I said the same thing: "I haven't had time." Richard would then suggest to me (rather annoyingly), that the truth was I hadn't made time.

It got to the point where I was going over to collect money from Richard, and I knew he was going to ask me about the book. So, I had no choice but to at least skim through the pages and read some of it.

That evening I arrived home late, as usual, and my family was in bed. I warmed up my dinner and sat down to read the book. As soon as I read the first few pages, I became hooked. I was reading a story about all my problems. I couldn't believe it. I stayed up and read the whole book from front to back cover without pausing for breath. I went to bed feeling the same excitement I had on the first day I started my business. Full of enthusiasm. Full of hope and possibility. It was an amazing feeling.

I bounced out of bed the next morning and proudly claimed, "I've got it!" to my long-suffering wife and daughters. I saw the look on their faces; they'd heard it all before. But as always, they listened to me talk about systems, processes, and delegation with the same support they always gave me.

When I got to see Richard, I brought him a bottle of red wine, and he knew I'd read the book. He smiled and welcomed me in. We spoke for hours about his business, coaching, how he read books and learned from them. He said, "You have to learn before you can earn." Another breakthrough mindset moment for me. If I learn more, I'll earn more. Of course—it's so obvious when you hear it.

I'd dropped out of school early to take a landscaping job because I didn't enjoy the academics, the learning, the systems of school life. Education was something I'd run away from—reading, personal development, mental growth. I'd replaced all that with learning hands-on skills. But Richard recommended two things that altered the course of my life, and he'll never know how much those two things have changed for me. For my family. For my team members. For my clients and mentees.

He said, "Read a book a week and get yourself a business coach."

We went on to discuss the impossibility of being good at everything or having enough time to learn it all. How there are great people in the world looking for opportunities, who are better than you are at the thing you're struggling with. I took his advice, and now I'm sharing it with you.

Right now, you probably won't appreciate the cumulative effect of reading for one hour every day. But if you do, it's going to put your business and personal life on to a level you can only dream about. I've read hundreds of business books and learned so much from all of the authors. Think about it. Some of the world's most successful people have written books about how they achieved their success. Revealed the secrets to their fortunes. All of it condensed down into one week of reading.

That one week of reading will give you 20 years or more of their knowledge. Apply the learning to your business, and you'll see changes happening before your eyes. Once you read something, the learning stays with you forever. And that's why I recommend reading consistently, even when it doesn't feel like you're taking it all in.

You can't unlearn something

I made some significant mistakes concerning learning and had preconceptions that I later discovered were false. On the very first day of primary school, I cried at the gate for my Mum to pick me up. I thought she'd gone and wasn't coming back. It's understandable then that I had a mental block between my feelings and learning, which was never addressed by anyone, including myself. As a result, I left school with zero qualifications and took on an entry-level job in a non-regulated industry—landscape gardening.

At school, I had no desire to learn and no passion for academics; I wanted to go to work and make some money. This wasn't my fault exactly; it was in my DNA. It was part of growing up in a working-class family with a dad who worked seven days a week.

However, today I love learning because I have a purpose for it and a release. I see the bigger picture that learning offers. Your personal development is so important in making sure you have a future to look forward to.

Physically, I knew I wasn't going to be able to keep working on the tools into my sixties, nor did I aspire to. But if all I knew was how to build a garden, how was I ever going to retire or even step back and enjoy life a little?

I have a pattern for learning that serves me very well. It's split into two categories, to make sure I'm getting the right level of input from both sides yet not taking in too much at once.

Category one is my longer-term learning. I'm

consistently reading every day on different subjects to improve my overall abilities and be an effective business owner. I never go for the latest shiny object; I always drink deep from classic books—the books that stand the test of time.

Category two is rapid, impact learning. This intense learning is on a subject I'm passionate about, such as direct response marketing, sales closing, and copywriting. Those three subjects fascinate me and keep me pushing to be better every day.

I learned early on in my development that you never stop learning, and you can never unlearn anything. This is helpful when you're taking on board new ideas and knowledge, but equally is unhelpful when you're trying to forget old, flawed learnings and overcome failures.

It's often the old chestnuts like, 'Money is the route of all evil,' and 'Good things don't happen to people like me,' that prevent you from topping up on the helpful learning you need to progress in life.

My tip is to use audiobooks for more inspirational, motivational, and feel good learning, and physical books for the impact learning so you can highlight sections and revisit them after you've finished.

Most importantly, when you learn something, take meaningful action. You don't have to know everything. In the beginning, you can make up in effort and commitment what you lack in knowledge.

What's a doer?

What's the point in all the learning if you don't act on what you learn?

But so many don't. On average, in a room of 1,000 people, only around 2% of them will take any action on the training they've done or the things they've learned. Most people genuinely intend to act, but it just never happens. You could call it fear of failure (we'll come to that later); however, it's fundamentally a lack of effort, an unwillingness to go the extra mile and get it done. And believe you me, this happens at every level of business.

I've always been a doer. Part of my problem was being a doer. Like I said earlier, we're both the number one problem and the number one solution in our businesses. Being a doer is fantastic if you're doing the right things at the right time. Being a doer of the wrong things means you'll be doing the wrong things faster, and effectively rocketing yourself to bankruptcy. Not to worry, it happens to the best of us—even the elite level marketing masterminds.

> *We even have something called the 'Barry Quotient' now: It's a scale on following through and implementing the ideas you receive in our group.*
> **~ John Carlton, the most ripped-off and respected copywriter alive**

The first day I arrived at the elite-level mastermind meeting in Phoenix, Arizona, I felt like a fish out of water, but I remember thinking I'd put in extra effort to compensate for my lack of knowledge. That entire first mastermind group meeting was scary, but I left with a clear set of goals, and the group gave me tremendous clarity. I went away to write my first book.

When I arrived in Boston, Massachusetts, four months later, with the book in my hand, the group were suitably impressed. It was then I realised we all need the same thing. We all need to be held accountable for our results. Even the highest paid, elite-level masterminds won't achieve without peer pressure, without accountability.

So, being a doer in a world of talkers gives you the edge. Most can talk the talk, yet very few walk the walk. If you can make up in effort what you lack in experience and knowledge, you'll always be putting one foot in front of the other. If you blame your circumstances or any other external factors, you'll always be one step forward, two steps back. All these concepts were new to me and coming at me thick and fast, but I wanted to grow, so I pushed myself out of my comfort zone.

The comfort zone thing

In principle, this is relatively easy to understand; in reality, it's an ongoing battle. The comfort zone you're operating in may be preventing you from moving forward, and it may be tricking you into a false sense of security.

I'll use an example I think is easy for everyone to understand. Remember the day you got your first house? The feeling of having this big monthly commitment would have been weighing heavily on your shoulders. You would've been feeling anxious and excited but also a little under pressure. That feeling was stretching you out of your comfort zone. And it was going out of your comfort zone that made it possible for you to get the house you wanted. Then, once you're in the house, you slide back into your comfort zone again, which is where the real danger lies.

Most people will get the house they always wanted and then fall into a comfort zone trap of not doing what's necessary to stay in the house. Often you push yourself to the limit to achieve success, then settle back again afterwards. But that loss of momentum can bring you right down to earth with a bump.

Panic sets in, and you start talking yourself into taking a step back or committing errors you weren't making when you were at full steam. Stay on track and keep driving on. Professional boxers say it's easier to win a world title than it is to defend one because the hunger is different. But in truth, whether they're defending it or not, they're still fighting for a world title.

Our mind is a funny thing, and we so readily let slip the practices that have got us all our success. Just the simple discipline of sticking to what's working is often enough. Tomorrow never comes. I knew once I got my business to function (on the whole) without me being around to handle the day to day work, I had to put systems in place to stay there. Not just processes, but the correct mindset as well. It's so easy to stop doing what's working. Why do we do that?

There are two signs I look for to determine if I'm in/out of my comfort zone. The first one is putting something off until tomorrow that I have enough time to do today. It's often my tell-tale sign of slipping into a comfort zone. The second is when I'm making changes, and it gets so uncomfortable, I feel like going back to how things were.

When I experience either of these reactions, I know it's a feeling of comfort, and I remind myself why I need discipline and why I'm making changes. That's enough to get over the initial feeling; then it passes, and I have the energy to keep going.

I'm a perfectionist

No, you're not. You're procrastinating. I've been a victim myself, as recently as today, getting ready to do the second edit of this book. I could so easily have put this off until tomorrow. Thankfully, I'm aware of the signs and push through them.

But what is procrastination in its simplest form? Often, people use the term 'I'm a perfectionist' when they're running behind or can't get something finished. In my experience, there's a thin line between perfectionism and procrastination. People who claim to be perfectionists are the same people who want everything and want it now. Procrastination is the guarantee. You want to be sure all the work you put in is going to be worth it.

When you go into anything new, you want to have a degree of certainty it's all going to benefit you in some way. I spent the first few months working with my coach on overcoming this. "You're procrastinating," my coach used to say. "You're going to need to be more determined. Stop saying you'll do it tomorrow." I didn't get it at first, because some things *had* to wait. BUT he meant the things that can't—slight hesitations that cause avoidable delays (typically involving payments).

Ironically, it costs us every single time we procrastinate, which is why this is such an important habit to identify in yourself. Developing the self-awareness to know when you're procrastinating is crucial. It's so easy to do; so easy to fall into the trap. Procrastination is one of the primary reasons coaching exists—so there's someone to keep pushing you when you want to slack off.

People frequently procrastinate at crucial development moments. Often on the big decisions, like hiring staff, taking on new business premises, or buying equipment and vehicles. These are just some examples.

I have a very recent story myself to illustrate the point. I was going through a recruitment process to find a marketing assistant for my landscaping business. At the beginning of the process, we identified the type of person we were looking for and the hours that person would be working. During the recruitment, we found a candidate who far exceeded our requirements, had a better skill set, and gave us much better options. A no-brainer you would think. Not so simple in reality.

We figured out how it would work internally, and I promised to get back to the candidate by Friday latest. On Friday we let the candidate know we needed a little more time to decide, even though we'd made a decision already. On the Monday, I had an emergency I had to take care of, which meant the candidate was still unsure of their position. Again, even with the emergency, I could have sent the message but was procrastinating.

I knew the candidate was very keen to come on board and take up the newly formed role, and the next morning, I started to write out a proposal for the position. Before I had a chance to send the offer, I received an email from the candidate saying, "I would like to withdraw from the process." After digging deeper into the reason why it became clear it was purely because of my hesitation. I hadn't taken the time to think it through properly or get it clear in my head, and my procrastination cost me an ideal hire.

That's one example of hundreds I could talk to you about. An illustration of a less important nature would be continually checking on holiday prices hoping you'll get the one you want for less, and your delays ultimately costing you more. I thought most of my flaws came from a lack of confidence, but then I discovered it wasn't confidence at all. I was looking for certainty, and I found it in the most unlikely of places. Let me explain.

Confident about not being confident

"I don't have any confidence," a business owner said to me once.

"Tell me about it," I said.

He went on to explain how he didn't have the confidence to increase his prices. Every time he tried, he lost the job, because people won't pay those prices etc. So, I offered to help with the problem, and if he came on board as a client, I would fix the confidence issue immediately. There and then. He said, "If you fix the issue right now, I'll join."

So, I began asking the questions:

"You're not confident you can sell the work at those prices?" I asked.

"No," the client said.

"You're not confident you can help your customers see the value in the prices?"

"No."

"And you're not confident about being able to build this business to the level you want?"

"No."

I said, "You sound pretty confident about having no confidence."

Here's the thing; most of us have the confidence; we just don't have the certainty it will work. If you knew something was going to work and you had a cast-iron guarantee, you wouldn't need confidence, just certainty. The certainty comes from a proven system. A proven track record, knowing someone has already trodden the path you want to tread. Entrepreneurs try something first; the rest try when it's proven.

I've been fortunate to spend decades working with and around high achievers who seem to possess superhuman abilities to identify and accomplish big goals. Barry, however, is in a class by himself.
~ Shawn Twing, Founder, Barn Door Media, LLC

It's madness to believe opportunities aren't all around us. We're all capable of taking advantage of the opportunities we have; the difference is some of us need certainty it will work before we take the risk. Others take the risk to create certainty. But here's the reality—it's all risky. Being first is risky. Being second is risky. Not doing it is risky.

Next time you have an opportunity, and you feel the fear, ask yourself this, "Do I need confidence right now, or am I looking for certainty?" Once you have certainty, you just need to commit yourself to it. I learned to dive right in and never rely on motivation.

Motivation is a myth

Personally, I've never believed in motivation. I think it's something people use as an excuse not to be committed to themselves or the task in hand; a way of accepting the failure of something before it's even started. If I had a pound for every time someone's said they lost motivation while working on a project, I could buy my own island.

A team leader in my landscaping company once missed a deadline on a project we were running, and I said, "What's stopped you getting this project finished?" The answer brought home to me why motivation is a myth: "The project was harder than we anticipated, and I had a challenge keeping the lads motivated."

Interestingly, when I suggested we have two separate wage structures (one for hours the team *are* motivated and one for hours the team *aren't* motivated), they didn't think it was a great idea. Now tell me motivation isn't a myth.

Motivation is superficial; it doesn't last. If you find yourself lacking motivation, you really need to look at your goals, your core purpose for what you're doing. Because the chances are you're playing too small. Your goals aren't big enough. The reason 'why' isn't big enough.

You need to be inspired; you need that feeling in the pit of your stomach where you'll do it or die. No matter what. Everyone has a thing that drives them, which is why we use vision boards and goal setting.

Set goals that scare you, I kept hearing. Everything scares me! I didn't want to mess anything up. It was easier to set small goals I would achieve than big goals I could miss. I didn't realise at the time, but I was worried about failing at business and life. So, I did some research, and I found there's a place in our minds we all go when we set huge goals. Just another mindset challenge to overcome.

Somewhere too scary for the average person to ever venture into.

Kakorrhaphiophobia. Where's that?

At some level, everyone fears failure.[1] It could be as simple as looking stupid on camera doing a live video on Facebook, or it could be as life-changing as losing your home. Whatever it is, we all have a fear of failure. So much so, that fear of failure can come disguised as a big personal goal.

See, having a big goal out in front of you can stop you doing the next thing next. When you fear failure, you procrastinate. So, you must break down the goal into small parts. Let me ask you this: How do you clean an elephant?

(The original saying is how do you *eat* an elephant, but my writing coach, Vicky, loves elephants, so I changed it to clean. Same principle, though, so it still works.)

Imagine if you had to clean an elephant—you wouldn't do it in one sitting, you'd do it a section at a time. Achieving your business goals is no different.

Don't look at your plans to build a team of ten employees as:

- Finding ten employees
- Raising the money for the vehicle and tools
- Finding the work for a bigger team
- Whether you're good enough to run a business that size
- Whether there are good people in the marketplace
- And all the other scary thoughts…

Just do the next thing next. Get stuck into the next task. If the next task is to hire a landscaper, then focus on that one task. When you push everything else to one side and just focus on the next thing, it's a whole lot easier to control your emotions.

When I feel backed into a corner, and I want to overcome the fear of failure—not just for my team and me, but with clients, mentees, and their teams—I ask myself two questions:

1. What's the worst thing that can happen?
2. If that happens, will I be able to get past it?

The answer is always yes to both questions. Despite all

the fears and what-ifs, I know by answering those two questions, I can confidently push on and do the next thing.

It hasn't always been like this. I've had employees who walked all over me because I feared they would leave if I challenged them. I've paid bonuses to people who didn't deserve it, just to keep a happy, harmonious workplace. I've accepted poor performance and attitude because I feared my business falling apart but accepting those things is pulling it apart anyway.

It all comes from the fear of failure. I wasn't the first to feel it, and I certainly won't be the last. But instead of facing my demons, I'd go and pick holes in what others were doing. It stopped me from feeling inferior, or like a failure, which made me feel a little better—for a while—about not dealing with my own problems.

Nobody has it easy, despite what it looks like from the outside. You can allow your fears to take over, or you can refuse to let them control you. It's all a mindset. Believing it's all going to fall apart, or someone has it easier than you, isn't serving you properly. Comparison is the thief of joy, and it makes us bitter too.

It's not just about us overcoming the fear of failure; it's also about us comparing ourselves unfavourably and becoming small-minded about other people and their success. There's a fine line between envy and mudita[3]; make sure you know which side your future self wants to be on.

Comparison is the thief of all joy

There will always be someone who appears to be doing better than you are. Just remember it's your journey, and for every journey, there's a bunch of things that could be better. This works in a few ways.

Firstly, it rears its ugly head with team members sabotaging the business success because they believe—often falsely—you don't care about them anymore. You may also get team members who think you're a millionaire because you now have a handful of lease-hired vehicles, or family members who think you've changed because you've developed a new mindset.

Secondly, you'll have moments when you question your success against the person you aspire to be like. Depending on where you're starting from, it may take you a while to get out of a negative financial position and into a positive one. So don't get disheartened if the person you're aiming to imitate is moving away from you. It's nice to think they're clearing a path for you to follow later, so the further away they get, the more opportunities they're presenting you with.

Something to watch out for is comparing yourself to others. If you ever find yourself doing this—stop. It's a bit of self-doubt and lack of self-belief; your inner critic creeping in.

We all love a bit of recognition, especially external acknowledgement. I find this is important to almost everyone I work with—even more so when the business is moving through the gears. However, it's hard to predict where the recognition will come from. Even, "Your business is doing well!" from your next-door neighbour (who you haven't spoken to before) can make you feel fantastic.

Let's look at the concept of comparison a little more deeply. I'd made the mindset shift from needing external recognition (an award, a thank you) to being internally satisfied (I know I've done a great job), and I was doing some research on internal and external recognition when I came across something on comparisons.

Once I'd investigated further, I started to watch out for the signs I'd learned about both in myself and other people. I was astounded by how much everyone repeats the same things.

Here are a few examples:

If your wife tells you John and Doris are going to Mexico in September, and your first response is not, "That's amazing, they deserve it!" you're comparing yourself and your achievements to theirs.

If your best friend tells you his brother is getting a Lamborghini and your first response is not, "What a fantastic achievement, I hope he loves every minute of driving it!" you're comparing yourself and your achievements to his.

If your next-door neighbour has a new TV delivered and your first response is not, "Good on them, they work hard and must be doing well" you're comparing yourself and your achievements to theirs.

These are all trifling examples, but you'll be amazed now I've highlighted it, just how much you're comparing yourself to others and causing more internal self-doubt. What you say to yourself matters as much as what you say to others, only it's at a deeper level. What we say has a massive influence on what we achieve. There's power in using the right language, as I found out through my management development.

The right words matter

The right words matter. A kick up the backside isn't necessarily physical; in fact, it's equally effective when it's verbal. The right words, at the right moment, for the right people, matter. Just like now—I can make my point in two ways, and so can you. One of them will get the wrong answer. By that I mean, it won't give you or the recipient any leverage to move forward.

Simple examples:

Why have you let your business get in such a mess?

Compared to:

What's stopped you from building a more successful business?

When you ask someone "why have you?" you always get a defensive reaction. And most people react rather than respond when under pressure. You have to choose your words carefully because the language you use often predetermines the response you get.

Slow things down. Stop dealing with your business and relationships at a surface level. Look at the core of the problem, not the problem itself. Everyone has deep-rooted issues they need to get to the bottom of before they can fix the problem. You do this by asking the right questions.

A lot of things don't make sense in business and life until we understand them. As soon as someone explains how, it's so obvious. It's happening all around you now, but you can't yet see it.

So, the people you employ will be feeling the same frustrations you do. They want to be something on the outside, but they have an internal person who is struggling to find the right words, perform the right actions, get the right results.

A caring conversation using the right questions helps them feel at ease, and you feel successful. To help others is very empowering, so dig a little deeper with your words. Like I said, a lot of things don't make sense.

Why would the most honest person tell white lies? Because we all fear rejection. "Why did you do that?" will never get you the answer you're looking for, and this is as true for adults as it is for kids. "How did that happen?" will always get you a more constructive answer to work with. You can then use the feedback to build in better systems for communication.

Likewise, don't give people the answer to the question. It's ok if the person in front of you is lost for words, or struggling to answer the question. They'll learn from it.

Another thing to be conscious of is not making requests when you expect results from a conversation. For example, never delegate something by saying, "I need you to complete this by 4 pm." Instead, say "I want you to complete this by 4 pm." Need is a requesting word, want is a demanding word. The words we use are a huge catalyst for the performance we get. Expectation and language must be congruent to achieve higher performance.

When you start asking yourself questions in a different way, you'll get different thoughts, and from there you'll get a different result for your business. If you believe you're exempt from this thinking, you're up the creek without a paddle.

Blame. Excuse. Denial

 Denial is not just a river in Egypt.
~ **Trevor 'ToeCracker' Crook**

I'm going to show some brutal love here, because you are the biggest problem in your business and in your personal life—and I think you know it. Don't even start building your company until you have a plan to build yourself. This is hard, I know, because you may be in denial about your problems.

It's true. How difficult is it right now to accept that you are the only reason you're not as successful as you think you should be? That you are the reason your business is harder to run than it should be? It's tough. Really tough. But unless you accept there's a problem, how can you ever fix it? Unless you're able to see there's a better way, why would you change?

Denial will hold you back, but once you accept you're the problem, you can overcome it. It's as simple as admitting it—you don't have to do anything else. You'll instantly grow as a person, although I must warn you, the minute you accept it, you'll find yourself in excuse land. And in excuse land, we never have enough time to get things done, our suppliers offer poor service, and our team members don't commit themselves enough.

Let me explain what's actually happening here. We move from being in denial to having excuses, only this time we're using external excuses. Taking away our external excuses leaves us with only ourselves to blame. Although we could still blame the people we expect to have more common sense, which is usually our team members. If that's true, (which it may well be), I'd ask you, "Who's responsible for the team members you've hired?" It's all a matter of acceptance. You accept there are no excuses, and blame disappears.

Yet still we blame our staff, our upbringing, the weather. We'd blame anyone and anything not to accept we are the problem. It's always us. Look, this is not a beat you up session, it's a get real one. Absolutely nothing is impossible to solve in your business if you first stop denying there's a problem.

When you get out of denial, accept no excuses, and stop blaming everyone for your results, you can move on. You are truly responsible for everything and anything in your business and life. How amazing is it to realise you can change everything? You'll have to have some tough conversations. You'll have to look yourself in the eyes and admit you messed things up, made bad decisions. These things aren't easy to do. You'll face some rejection, but so what? If you want to change you have to face it. And you really can change everything when you give up the fear of rejection.

The fear of rejection

What if they say yes?

The strongest of emotions in business, for me, is the fear of rejection. You're damned if you do and damned if you don't. Either the customer rejects the price, or the team rejects you for not making the sale. Same with recruitment. Sometimes you're rejecting people who want the position, which is not a nice thing to do, or the candidate rejects the offer, which is a dent to your ego.

Wherever you turn you're in danger of rejection, and that's hard to deal with. Especially if you're in a position where you want to hire a coach for your business, for example. If I hire the coach and it goes wrong, I'll suffer ridicule. If I hire the coach and I can't do the work, I'll look stupid. If I tell my family I'm hiring a coach they'll think I've failed. If I don't hire a coach, I might go bankrupt.

Damned if you do, damned, if you don't... although I'd personally prefer to take the risk of hiring a coach and not succeeding than not hiring one and never knowing if I would have succeeded or not. Like my favourite sports stars, Roger Federer and Manny Pacquiao. Both need coaches, trainers, nutritionists, sports scientists, sports psychologists. You name it, they hire them.

Why? Because these experts see what you don't. They help you grow as a person as well as an athlete. They help you see the lessons in loss, rather than the loss itself. Everyone on every level has a fear of rejection; you aren't unique in that sense. But the people who grow fastest understand there are lessons to be learned in rejection.

Raise those prices. Hire those people. Book those trips. You will make it. You just have to believe you will before you can see it. That takes a little courage, but without a change in thinking, you won't see a change in your fortunes.

For things to change, you must change

For things to change, first you must change. That's the way I opened this book. It's the message that brought me to this point right now; I have no doubt about it. But why do people find it so hard to change? And why do people expect change to be immediate? We all have diverging thresholds to change.

Some people are super uncomfortable with change; others are more uncomfortable when there's no change for a long time. Neither is correct, nor incorrect. The only thing that's wrong is not to change when you need to. It's fundamentally quite simple; if something isn't giving you the result you want, it has to change.

Which is obvious, but it takes people too long to make the change. Precisely why the message made me see things differently. I was repeating the same mistakes over and over again. I knew I had to make changes, I just didn't know how to. I wasn't sure where to start. I was always of the belief "Next week it will be better," or "Just get this week out of the way, and things will improve."

It never did get better. Now I know why. Now *you* know why.

If you want to change anything, it has to come from

you first. I had to change myself before I could change anything else. I had to see things differently before I could evolve.

Change is hard but staying the same is harder. If you repeat the same actions expecting different results, you're as batshit crazy as I was. It was torture, and I was the person creating it.

There's a lesson in there somewhere. We all learn most from mistakes.

There's always enough time to correct mistakes

Who, honestly, enjoys making mistakes? No one seriously relishes getting things wrong, but here's the thing… all of our best lessons come from making mistakes. In fact, you learn nothing from things going well, other than it went well. It isn't enough for you to dig into the reason why it went well—just accept it did and move on.

That's because some people need to feel the pain to realise something needs to be different. But, again, there's a lesson in this too. How quickly do you want to get the pain out of the way? I consider failing fast—or making mistakes fast—among the top five things that have changed my life. The faster you make mistakes, the quicker you get to the answer.

Perfection is great in a hypothetical world, but none of us lives in one of those. Perfection is, in reality, just a form of procrastination (I think I've said that already!) No one has time to make things perfect. You already admit you don't have enough time to do the day to day work in your business, never mind developing the new processes and training you need for your team.

You can't deny this; after all, no matter how busy you are, if an irate customer calls with a complaint, you drop everything to go and fix the problem. Always happens. So, to me, if you can forever find the time to fix mistakes—and customers are eternally grateful to you for fixing mistakes —you should be making them as fast as possible.

You'll always find the time to fix mistakes in your business and personal life, but you'll never, *never*, NEVER find the time to sit and perfect something before the world sees it.

Stop looking for perfection and start looking for progress. Everything is a decision away from being fixed. I had to choose, and someday, maybe today, you will have to choose too.

The ball's in your court

You can often be pushed into decisions by mediocre employees or customers who expect way more than they're prepared to pay for, which makes you feel you're in a position of helplessness. But in truth, everything is your choice.

You could, if you really wished, close the door on your business tomorrow and set off in a new direction. I know you're thinking you have bills to pay—I get it. But are you going to remain a slave to that forever?

I'm not suggesting you close the door. I'm simply showing you you're not trapped. You have choices—like I had when I met my coach. Any sensible human being would have started again, but I didn't (I wish I had now). Not literally; I just didn't choose to start again mentally. It felt like I would be quitting on the hard work I had already committed to.

I'm the perfect example of becoming a product of my environment. I grew up amongst proud men, who would rather die than admit failure. Even given a choice to start again, I chose to roll my sleeves up and go through the swamp to prove how tough I was.

I don't regret that now, I'm at peace with it; but it could have been easier. I could have learned from my mistakes quicker. I didn't need to repeat the same things over and over before seeing the error of my thinking.

And all of this is about the way we choose to think about our future. If we decide today to go in a new direction, we can. Nothing is holding us back; nothing. Not even our expenses, our bills, or our debts.

When you're ready to choose an easier path, you can. So, I wanted to end this chapter by reminding you of this:

For things to change, you have to change first.

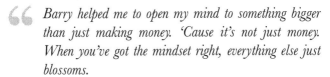

Barry helped me to open my mind to something bigger than just making money. 'Cause it's not just money. When you've got the mindset right, everything else just blossoms.
~ **Craig McGibbon, London**

Summary

I'd never read a business book before, yet somehow, I found myself reading one book that changed the course of my life. It was completely out of my comfort zone, and what I was reading scared me and excited me in equal measures.

I know now, I have an inherent fear of failure—I doubt that will ever change, which is why *I* had to. I took action even when I wasn't sure it would all work out, and ended up in an elite business mastermind group in America.

I figured out you can make up in effort what you lack in knowledge, at any level of business. You don't get given anything. If you have an insatiable work ethic, take action on what you learn, and focus on doing the next thing next, you can make big things happen.

Lesson 1

If you want a different result, you must take different actions.

When you're ready to understand how to make the change, head over to www.barryrandall.co.uk/booklessons and watch the video: **for things to change, first you must change...**

————————————————————

1. That's what kakorrhaphiophobia means: the intense fear of failure.

2

MONEY IS A TOOL

How Your Money Story May Be Holding You Back

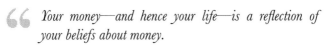 *Your money—and hence your life—is a reflection of your beliefs about money.*
~ Ken Honda

H ere's where it all begins…

I grew up in a real working-class family on a fairly rough council estate in the centre of Leicester. All the men worked seven days a week, and the ladies were housewives with good broods of children.

My dad worked a job in a factory, and back then, he would get two weeks off work at the beginning of July—what we called the 'July Fortnight.' While other kids at school went on holiday, my dad would work on the bins to earn some extra money. It was an old-fashioned set up in today's world, but it worked, and everyone was always happy.

The boys in each household typically left school to work with their dads or in the same trade. They adopted the same characteristics, drank in the same pubs, and essentially became a clone of their father. I say this from experience because I grew up with three younger brothers:

Jeff, who is two years younger than me; Lee, who is five years younger than me; and Tom, who is 12 years younger than me. All of us went on to do landscape gardening.

I left school at 15 with no qualifications and took a low-paid landscaping job with an old guy called Bill Pollard. I think he was 75 at the time and still lifting old 3x2 paving slabs until the day he quit. My dad also worked for him and eventually went on to run the business until the recession destroyed it in the late nineties.

Of course, being institutionalised to a point, I grew up with the same beliefs, the same values, and the same mindset as my Dad and others before him. One of the things that I settled into quickly was working seven days a week. People told me, "If you want to make more money you need to put in the hours and work weekends." Fine by me. I just got on with it, and it wasn't uncommon to be called a workaholic even at a young age.

I would work hard all week, and at the weekend I'd buy my girlfriend, Marie, (who is now my wife) new shoes, or a coat, or some perfume, and then spend the rest of the money on 'having a good time'. I was quickly becoming part of the system and falling into line. Becoming a younger version of my dad, and that felt great to me.

I would speak to my dad about my ambition to be a singer or be in a band. I wanted to have the luxuries life had to offer, and I used to read articles about auditions in London to join bands and wonder if it was for me. In truth, I can't sing a note in tune, but I'm very, very driven, so nothing was going to stop me! I'll get to that later.

For a while, I was laughed at and put off the idea. I'd have people saying things like, "As long as you've got a few quid for a drink at the weekends that's all you need," and for at least 20 years, I was torn between believing it and wanting more.

It wasn't wrong of these people to mock and laugh; it was all they knew. But I also knew they had no pensions, no savings, and no long-term plans; and anyway, I wanted a Lamborghini. Of course, I wasn't going to get that with no cash in the bank, was I? And without cold hard cash, the only thing any of us can rely on is the belief we'll get there in the end… wherever there is.

You are what you believe you are

The lack of money in your account right now is not your fault.

Your level of income and savings is a reflection of your beliefs about money and how easy it is to come by. So a dismal bank balance usually means an unsatisfactory relationship with money. All money is a matter of belief.

The key to wealth is to make your money work for you, rather than you work for it. It's what you do with the money you earn rather than the amount of money you earn that determines your financial position.

But why is that? It's an excellent question to ask yourself.

When we're growing up, we're subjected to other people's beliefs about money. None of us is born with a preconception about the value of our time or a cap on our earning potential. We develop this through others. Depending on who you're receiving advice from, you'll have a perceived value of money.

We've all heard someone else say, "Money won't make you happy," or "Money is the root of all evil," and these statements/beliefs are ingrained in us when we're growing up. So, it's going to have a negative effect on you, especially when you're giving customers prices. When you have an unhealthy relationship with money, and you believe it doesn't make you happy, it shows up in your bank account.

Those memories stay with you and put you under pressure when you're selling work to prospects. It creates a scarcity mindset around money, and often a belief that there's not enough out there for you to be comfortable. But people like you do make a lot of money.

People with misplaced beliefs about money undercut themselves on prices and take on jobs they don't ideally want. Then they spend a few weeks stuck on the job earning a small amount of money when if they'd waited, a better job would have come along.

We all know it's better to have a day or two empty in our diary than be tied up for two weeks on a low paying job. At least we can spend some time with our family in those two days. So, why do we still take on the work and let ungrateful customers make us feel like they're doing us a favour? Easy. Flawed beliefs about money that we've picked up from our elders as we were growing up.

I didn't always think like this. I used to fill my work diary at any cost. I thought having ANY work in the diary was better than having none. Until I knew my business numbers inside out, I worked too hard for nowhere near enough. I'm convinced it changed the day I had a particular conversation with my coach.

He asked me what I did with the money I earned. Not the business's money, the bit I took for myself. So, I explained about the mortgage, food, utilities, and old debt repayments.

Then he said, "What about the bit that's left?"

"I'm not sure where that all goes," I replied.

Then he said, "Do you think it's a good idea to not know where it all goes?"

I said, "I'm not sure what you mean."

"Maybe you should," he said.

From that day forward, I started to watch what I did with my money. The bit left after I'd paid the essential bills. I didn't change all my spending habits but knowing what I was spending the money on made it last longer. In fact, watching it made me appreciate it more. Until then, I'd felt I needed to earn more to have more.

Once I'd got my head around money management, I began investing some of it. Only a small amount—£250 per month. The decision to invest it led to a meeting with my financial advisor, Tim, who showed me what was possible through compound interest. I've produced a small example for you below, which I've taken from the calculatorsite.com.

ISA 10-year plan

Initial balance: £500

Interest rate: 5% per year (it could be more depending on your risk profile)

Monthly deposit: £500 (you pay £500 per month into the ISA)

Annual inflation: 5% (you increase what you put in by 5% each year)

At the end of the ten years, you'll have £96,940.70

If you wanted to invest more, and over a longer period, it makes a significant difference.

ISA 20-year plan

Initial balance: £500

Interest rate: 5% per year (it could be more depending on your risk profile)

Monthly deposit: £1,000 (you pay £1,000 per month into the ISA)

Annual inflation: 10% (you increase what you put in by 10% each year)

At the end of the 20 years, you'll have £1,014,978.85

Now this book isn't about financial planning; I just wanted to show you the change I had in mindset around money. The pressure comes from trying to turn our lives around immediately, but this shows it's better to get rich slowly than try to get rich quickly. After all, if you could find the £1,000 per month to invest in an ISA from next month and did so for 20 years, you'd have over £1 million!

Try it for yourself. Go and reach out to a financial advisor and start a long-term savings plan. The feeling of preparing for the future will ease your anxieties around investment. Most anxieties come from fear of the future, but if done correctly, a savings plan takes care of the financial insecurity.

Investing doesn't have to involve large sums of money. You can start modestly and build as the business does. Using the tables above, even starting with £250 per month over 20 years will pay out £254,084.50, with the compounded effect of interest. I know 20 years seems a long time, but it will eventually pass, and you won't miss the £250.

Time is your number one currency

This section is about you. Taking what you're worth. Putting pressure on yourself to make it work. When you increase how much you take from the business, you'll make different decisions about how you spend your time.

Simple but scary advice often works. I read a book called *Profit First: Transform Your Business from a Cash-Eating*

Monster to a Money-Making Machine by Mike Michalowicz, and it was the first time the concept of paying myself had dawned on me. I was always able to find the money for the bills, but never to pay myself. I kept thinking, if I leave everything I earn in the business, it will eventually come back to me. It never did.

When I changed to paying myself first, I no longer had the money for the supplier bills. That put enormous pressure on me—much greater pressure than when the money wasn't there for me. I wasn't sure how I would overcome the challenge, but I did. I had to do things differently to ensure the money came in for the supplier bills and staff wages.

I started using this simple checklist:

- Spend more time checking in on the running projects
- Pay closer attention to the planning of each project
- Make small increases to my labour prices and material mark up
- Demand less wastage of material on-site
- Make cutbacks on all my overheads (except marketing)
- Start doing one-to-one meetings with my key team members

As soon as I made a shift in thinking concerning my finances, I recovered the wage I'd denied myself without doing any additional turnover. It was there all along, but I wasn't focusing on it; I clearly didn't value my own time as much as I valued everyone else's time.

Setting up a long-term retirement plan is no different. You don't wait to retire; you plan to retire. You start today and meet retirement when you get to it. Everything you're doing is a plan, and you should be designing the perfect life, not having it happen by accident. You are the number one asset in your business.

All of this starts with you understanding the value of your time—not the *price* per hour, the *value* per hour. But, just like a lot of people I meet in this industry, you probably had bad money advice growing up. Remember I got told if you want more money, just work weekends? And I did?

I'm not a big fan of working weekends. I do it. Of course, I do it. Doesn't mean I enjoy it. Yet when I was starting out in business, I worked every weekend to build up my diary and bank account (which I didn't do very well, as you know). My dad always told me if you want to earn more money, work weekends, which is very true—you do earn more by working weekends than by not working weekends. But in the context of being a business owner, working weekends is not a leverage tool; it's a short-term solution to a longer-term profit problem.

Simple things like, how do you plan for Monday if you're working Sunday? Because kicking off a new week without a solid plan is going to cost you way more than you can earn on a single Sunday on-site. And let's face it, we're not as committed on a Sunday as we are in the week. For a start, we always run out of material on a Sunday and nowhere's open, which adds to the pressure you've put yourself under.

In the beginning, I used weekends to do smaller projects and build up my bank account, so I could get some tools and a vehicle, ready to launch my business. I wish I'd known more about marketing and coaching then. Once the business was running and I had employees, I was doing the weekends just to placate customers with urgent start dates and catch up on schedules when the team was falling behind.

All this thinking was down to my belief in trading my time for money. Now I trade money for time. If I invest in additional support, I get more time at home with my family. People ask how I can run my business on seven hours of meetings each week, and the answer is straightforward: I pay for the privilege. Yes, I could earn more if I took on a lot more responsibility myself, but how much is enough?

Money is not your biggest asset; time is. You can always earn more money, but you can't get the time back that you lose from managing your business badly and running yourself into the ground. However, it's not easy to change the habit of a lifetime. All business owners in the landscaping industry start their careers working for a low hourly rate or a low m^2 (square metre) rate. Understandably, we would see every hour worked as money earned.

But this simple mathematical equation should help you see the difference:

Barry wants to spend more time with his family, but only charges £40 per hour for landscaping work. He has a job to do, which is going to take 11 hours on Friday. He quotes the client £440.

Barry is doing the job himself, so he decides to hire someone to help him get the work done earlier. He employs Sue, whose rate is £10 per hour. With Sue on board, Barry should get the job done in around half the time (let's call it six hours).

Now, Barry is going to make £440 for the job, less Sue's £60, which gives him a total of £380. £380 for six hours works out to £63.33 per hour. So, he makes more money per hour doing less work and paying a member of staff. Plus, he gets the one thing he wants most—time with his family.

If you're super observant, you'll notice Barry could have made £440 by doing it himself. However, he's invested £60 in paying Sue to halve his workload and make time to see his family. Business and life are both about priorities; if you want more time, you'll have to pay for it. It took me a little while to get my head around the value of my time, but now I know how much it's worth, I'm considerably happier with what I'm earning.

Know your worth

I sold my first garden design for a fee of £99 and felt invincible. It was the first time I'd ever asked for money for a design. It also put me under pressure, though—pressure to deliver a great product. Until that point, I would design a client's garden for free because I wanted to do the landscaping work.

To me, the landscaping work was the chargeable work, so I always produced a drawing to convince them of the value. But with the benefit of hindsight, I was undervaluing the design, undervaluing myself, and avoiding asking for the design fee because I didn't believe in myself enough.

I only realised this when I got that first fee. I then felt pressure to get the design right as well as pressure to do the work. Those two feelings compounded were exciting—I liked the pressure.

As the years have gone on, I've been amazed at how many people do design work for free. Giving away all that intellectual property. Every one of them afraid to ask for a fee, just like I was. But where does this attitude come from? Why do we devalue our design skills? Is it just the design that we devalue?

I believe our self-worth and the value we place on ourselves all stems from earlier introductions to money. Things we picked up from our childhood, like the conversation we overheard our parents have. It's scarcity at the deepest level—a mindset where we fear losing out.

I'm convinced landscaping doesn't have a value. That in fact, it's worth only what a client is prepared to pay for it. With this mindset, I can set the price based on what I see as being my unique value in the marketplace. To that end, you or I can set our own rate. A rate we believe to be our worth. Then we simply tell the client what that is, not the other way around.

But—big but. I know every meeting you have, you'll feel like the client has a choice. This is where you must hold your prices and choose your clients, not the other way around. If you don't place a higher perceived value on yourself, your potential clients won't either. If you find yourself in negotiations with clients and reducing your labour rates to win jobs, it's only because you have a gap to bridge between what you want and what you feel you're worth.

Here's a simple exercise to check whether you're pricing your work at the rate you believe you're worth. If you got to the door of a prospect's house holding your design and quotation under your arm and the homeowner said, "Hi, I'm so happy to see you. We wanted you to do the job from the moment we met you. In fact, so much so we haven't asked anyone else to price for the work. It doesn't matter how much it is we're going with anyway."

Would you want to reprice the job and add more to the price? If the answer is yes, you're not charging enough, because you don't think it's possible to get the price you actually want. But you should, because you're worth it.

When you reach the point of knowing your self-worth, you gain control—control of what you charge for your time.

That brings control of your feelings… of your future… of everything.

Just to wrap this up, it's not the love of money that's the root of all evil, but the lack of money. More business owners suffer mental health problems from a lack of money than they do from an abundance of wealth. Whether your bank account is healthy or wretched, it's just a feeling.

Don't let those feelings control you as I let them control me.

Don't let money control you

No one makes enough money. Even the billionaires are trying to make more. So, what is money, and why do we want to make more? What are we doing it all for when we do? If you only have one goal in business—cash in the bank—and money only serves one purpose for you, you'll never quite get off the hamster wheel. Because money has multiple purposes and sculpts numerous personalities.

I follow a simple philosophy now, which I picked up reading a book by Jim Rohn called *The Day That Turns Your Life Around*. This philosophy has allowed me to control my finances better, given me security for the future, and made my money stretch further ever since. The advice is so beautifully simple: "Save first and spend what's left."

I used to live for the weekends. If you remember back, I followed what I had seen growing up. I even spent all my first week's pay on the Saturday morning. That pattern continued for almost 22 years. I'd have fantastic summers and awful winters because I lived for the weekend. If I earned twice as much this week as I had last week, I had twice as much to spend.

It's easy to convince yourself to do it. 'You only live once,' was more than enough to get me to spend everything I'd earned and go back out on Monday to do another shift. What I didn't realise is the mental pressure I placed on myself by not having money behind me for a rainy day. And it's almost inevitable that your car breaks down when you have no money in the bank. Never happens when you're flush, does it?

So, money, for me, isn't just cash in hand. It serves a lot of purposes and creates a lot of opportunities, but also causes a lot of problems. A lack of money can result in anxiety, poor decision making, resentment, and stress. An abundance of money gives you choices, makes you feel better and more laid back. But how much is enough? What would you do if you had plenty of money? How would you feel if money was never an issue again?

As you go through this book, think about it, and question yourself often: If money wasn't my challenge, what would I do differently? Who would I hire? What would I invest in?

Start thinking bigger. Instead of doing one thing after the other, do multiple things at once. I don't mean paperwork and phone calls. I mean various streams of income from different businesses. I used to do my work in a linear fashion. One thing after the other until I discovered leverage. It's possible to do sales, recruitment, and project management at the same time. Listen up.

Leverage level thinking

"Richard, where do I put my bags?"

Can you imagine how small Virgin Atlantic would be if

Richard Branson wanted to serve the drinks, board the passengers, and sell the holidays? And the same for Jeff Bezos, the Amazon head honcho. Do you honestly think Amazon would be able to do next-day delivery if he worked for himself?

You can't do everything yourself, and that's ok. Often you can't do it nearly as well as other people, and again, that's ok. If I had wanted to control every aspect of my business, I wouldn't be writing this book, I wouldn't have supported so many business owners, and I would still be on the tools.

In the essence of leverage, I was interviewing someone for a sales manager's position, so I could step down and allow the sales in my business to grow. During the interview, I asked a question that stopped me in my tracks. I asked, "Was your success down to you, or the team you had built around you?"

The answer to the question didn't need to come, I already knew; I already knew for her what was true for me. You don't build a great business; you build a great team. They build the business for you.

Did you know McDonald's makes more money from one simple question than all their other systems and advertising put together?

"Do you want fries with that?"

What else can you do for your clients that could make you more money by asking one simple question? A client of our Black Diamond membership asks this question: "Is there anything else we can help you with?" Made him £16,000 in one week. Interesting…

Does it need a super-skilled landscaper to ask the question? No. You can get anyone to do it for you. And there are people who would love to work for you. Love it. Is it sometimes easier to do things yourself than hire other people? Yes. Is it easy to ask someone to do something for you which you could easily do yourself? Yes.

Don't feel guilty for giving someone a great opportunity.

Someone needs an opportunity

My coach said, "As soon as your hourly rate allows you to, you should get yourself a cleaner." He wasn't being literal; it was to demonstrate a point. If you can earn £50 per hour running your business and you can get the car cleaned for £20, unless you are in love with cleaning the car, you should hire someone to do it for you. If you clean the car, you make nothing; if the valet cleans the car, you make £30 not to clean it.

It's a small example of exchanging your time for money. Maybe it's another illustration of fearing rejection because I found it fairly hard passing on tasks to someone that were easy for me to do myself.

When I was young, I'd often hear comments like, "What did your last slave die of?" and "Get off your backside and stop being lazy!" Comments like this sit deep in your memory and even make it difficult to tell someone to take the mail to the post box, for example.

That's still something I find difficult today. I have a fantastic assistant who delights in managing my diary, yet I still find it difficult to ask her to book my hair appointment for me. Could I easily make the call and sort that myself? Yes, absolutely. But I also have things in my diary that only I can do, which is the part I should be doing.

My assistant Helen isn't affected by my request; in fact, it's better if I ask her to make the appointment for me, so the diary doesn't get double-booked. Helen also makes sure all my invoicing, end of month accounts, and pretty much anything I need is always done for me so that I can concentrate on my income-generating tasks.

The point of this chapter is to emphasise how difficult it can be to hand over small tasks to an employee. Firstly, because you may see it as a cost, and secondly, you may see it as something personal to you. Trusting someone to do the work right is hard, and trusting yourself to hire the right person is harder. Trusting yourself to let go is hardest of all, but you can't get everything done by yourself.

Most of the work you end up doing when the business grows isn't income generating. In other words, it isn't something you can charge a client for. Sending invoices brings cash into the business, but it isn't income generating. Booking prospects into your diary keeps the work coming in but isn't income generating. Managing your social media channels is bringing leads in, but it isn't generating income.

If you're a landscaper, you only make money when you're on-site. You only have 24 hours a day, seven days a week, to do everything. If you're working 14-hour days and still not getting it all done, bring on board an assistant.

Hiring people to work with your finances requires trust. But who is it we don't trust? Ourselves or the team members? Trust is a big thing, which comes from our poverty and scarcity mindset. Let me tell you about mine and how I got over it.

If you have trust issues

I didn't trust anyone, but I trust everyone; which is complicated. More complicated than it sounds! The first person I hired where I felt completely out of control was my office manager Sue. Part of my fear was whether I knew enough to lead and manage her; the rest was handing over access to my bank account.

I felt so close to the business it was as if I was attached to it by an umbilical cord. There was no distinction between me personally and my company; in my eyes, they were the exact same thing, which made each decision HUGE. This level of emotional investment in your business clouds every decision you make. Getting an invoice wrong feels like you'll lose your house and your family will be out on the street. As crazy as that sounds, these thoughts affect us all.

The lead up to the first day was nerve-racking. I'd put no planning in place and kept thinking, "What's she going to do when she's here?" My focus wasn't on the office structure, so I saw it as just a few hours, even though it was keeping me away from my family all week.

The first week I diverted all calls to my mobile to make sure they got answered correctly and even collected the wages from the bank, put the cash into the envelopes, and gave them to Sue to hand out.

The following week Sue asked, "Why have I been hired?"

"To run the office," I replied.

"But you've diverted the calls and done the banking… that's what you hired me for!" Sue said. From that moment forward I realised, only by letting people in was I ever going to improve my working life.

Sue took on the office processes and day by day made my whole life easier. Timesheets, customer records, banking and accounting records, customer service calls, qualification calls. I quickly offloaded everything from my brain.

It was revolutionary. I felt completely liberated. All these things I thought only I could do properly were slowly driving me towards a nervous breakdown. I'm proud to say Sue is my Finance Manager now, and without her support, help, and guidance, the business would still be stuck in my head and, in all likeliness, closed.

Watch the pennies

Why do lottery winners go broke?

Fairly simple question. Does anyone know? I think I do. The money is bigger than the person. You can't increase your earning until you increase your learning. Which is why I said before that reading is vital to profits. I stand by that completely.

I remember meeting my financial advisor, Tim, for the first time. I rocked up in my pick-up truck and work clothes asking random questions about compound interest. How quickly will my money compound? When will I be able to take it out? Do I have to pay tax on it? I honestly had no idea what compound interest was, how it would help, or where to start.

But like most things in life, it all starts with taking the first step and building relationships. I met Tim, and at the time, I had about £50 per week to invest in a savings account. He talked me through investing and explained what some of the more technical terms meant. Like an ISA - I'm serious, I had no idea!

After our conversation, I left, and we spoke again a few weeks later. He said, "I don't work with many people who have such a small budget, but I can tell from talking to you, you're going to be successful." I started investing that £50 each week and never looked back. Since then, my investment portfolio has grown. The weekly investments have increased, and Tim is still my financial advisor today.

Loyalty is crucial in business, especially where finances and longer-term investing are concerned. It could be investing your cash in stocks and shares or investing it in training and development for your employees. The most important thing to remember is to start somewhere. Doesn't matter how small, doesn't matter how often; as long as it's consistent and focused on the long term.

It's easy to save to buy something. A little harder to save to gain something. In just over four years, my whole future has changed by investing a small percentage of what I earn into a long-term plan. Get started today. Most of our anxieties are fears of the future, and money is a big factor in that. Fix this problem by investing a small amount. You don't miss it, and once you get started, it becomes addictive.

Pay yourself first

I'm guilty of paying everyone else first and missing out myself. This one time, just before Christmas in 2010, when I was starting to venture into self-employed work, I got presented with a driveway project to complete.

At the time, I had four people who worked with me on and off. I wanted to build a business and employ them, but I wasn't anywhere near ready to start a proper company (that came along in 2012).

It was the week before Christmas, and I pulled these four people in to do a job with me. At the end of the week, the client paid me the £3,000, and I paid them all for the week plus a little bit as a Christmas bonus. That left me with nothing, but at the time, I wasn't too concerned because I wanted the guys to be happy and come back in and work with me in the new year. These people, I thought, would eventually become employees when I started my business.

We went off to the pub—as we did most Fridays—and all sat around talking about the year and what people had planned over Christmas, and I explained I'd like to start up the business properly in 2011. A few weeks later, I was talking to one of them individually and explaining how I'd given them everything from the job and left myself short over the holidays. He said, "I didn't realise you'd done that. None of us did. But one of the lads was moaning he hadn't been given more money as a bonus."

During the Christmas break, I was so broke I had to scrape together odd coins from the car, down the back of the sofa, and from coat pockets just to buy a newspaper. So, today, no matter what the business performance is, I make sure I get paid. Fortunately, I have amazing people around me who support my vision, but there's still some who will never get enough, no matter how much you give them.

Don't be afraid to share your successes and failures with your team members. If they're the right people for you, they'll want to see you doing well. I've never been comfortable talking about money, but it's my assumption that people will assume I'm entitled or arrogant that makes me defensive. I don't want to appear brash.

Sharing your successes might be the spark that helps someone else go on to achieve their dreams, which is why I decided to tell the world.

It's not bragging

I'm still uncomfortable about showing off my successes. Talking about money in front of the wrong people can seem like you're bragging. Though part of me wants to be open about what I've achieved, the other half believes I'm just rubbing it in people's faces.

There's a process to success which everyone has to go through. When you've scraped a few pennies together to get a newspaper at one point, then signed for and purchased a Bentley at another, you get to witness both sides of it.

I still don't think I've posted a picture of my car on social media. It was a long-time goal of mine to buy a Bentley Continental GT, and I'm still uncomfortable showing it off. I know why—when you grow up in a working-class environment and often live hand to mouth, you become frustrated at life and the apparent lack of opportunities available to you.

People who are successful and show off their wealth are classed as braggers and seen as stuck up, whatever that is. I know it's a faulty way to see the world, but it existed for me. You become more exposed to this mindset as your business grows, and the more you grow as a person. Although I still struggle with attitudes to wealth, I choose to talk about these issues as my story helps others.

It's this, and the pleas from family and friends for you not to change that's tough to let go of. Trying to hold on to both crushes your dreams. A lot of people are frightened you'll leave them behind or change too much. It's not true. You will change, absolutely, but it'll be for the better. Not just for you either—it benefits everyone around you.

I've been a personal goal setter for a long time and enjoyed achieving lots of my ambitions. One of the great things about my goal setting is my youngest daughter's exposure to success in her early years. When she was ten years old, I took her on a first-class flight to Florida, we stayed at the Waldorf Astoria, and I chauffeured her around in a Mustang convertible.

Now, she's disappointed if we're not flying business class. That doesn't make her a 'snob' (something else I would hear people say). It also doesn't make her 'ungrateful' (another word I would hear a lot). It just means she has high expectations of what she should be able to achieve in life.

If you experience finer living at an earlier age, you don't want to settle for anything less when you're older. Note to you and me: Share our successes, no matter what anyone else thinks. I wrote this on Friday 14th August 2020, and if you visit my Facebook page, you'll see I decided while writing it that I was finally going to post a picture of my Bentley and overcome the fear.

And, really, there's no reason not to share your successes, because you can't have success without hard work. It's the hard work that brings the profit. It also brings the tax bills... something I had an issue with until I was firmly put in my place by my coach.

You don't have a tax problem

I love paying my taxes, and the bigger they are, the better. By the way, this is a significant money mindset shift for any entrepreneur and business owner. No, I'm not crazy. Why should I fear a big tax bill? If I've got a big tax bill, it means I've made a lot of money. But I didn't always welcome big tax bills; in fact, I used to begrudge paying them.

I'm not one of these people who complains about how others get government support, yet small business owners get nothing. I'm much more of a 'paddle my own canoe' type of entrepreneur. Although, at every stage of the business's growth, I've had challenges around my liabilities. What I deemed to be fair, what it all meant to me, and how to get around it, over it, under it—the usual things.

The first one was going VAT registered. I'm not the only person to have these thoughts—most business owners I speak to who are approaching the VAT threshold want to know how to avoid it, or whether it will cost them work. The fear is more about the person's perception of cost than the client's expectation about paying VAT. Everyone knows tax exists, so it's not a surprise to anyone to have to pay it.

BUT the struggle is real. I remember approaching the threshold myself in year one of running my business—actually it was in the first four months, and it was scary! I was already losing work to competitors because they were cheaper than I was, and now I needed to add 20% to my prices. I'd already made the assumption it would cost me work and ultimately my business.

For the first month or so, I added the VAT but reduced the number of chargeable labour days, so I could keep my prices close to the pre-VAT levels. But that started to show in my month-end numbers and I had to change it. I had a real fear of increasing my prices by adding VAT. I put so much energy into worrying about the higher prices compared to the competitors I didn't once stop to think how much more professional it made me.

For the remainder of the first year, our sales rose rapidly (due in large part to my guarantee, which I'll talk about in the marketing chapter) and we ended year one with a turnover of £377,000. Being in a hurry to grow my business, I would continually be investing in new equipment, training for my team, and educating myself through coaching and seminars, which always made cash flow tight.

When the tax bills come around, it would always be a scraping the pennies together exercise to keep the wolves from the door. I'd have my hand down the back of the sofa, go weeks without pay, and sacrifice all sorts to get the money together to pay the tax. I never enjoyed those payments and would always complain about how much I'd already paid.

One day during another downbeat moment, my coach said to me, "It's true you've got a short-term cash flow issue, but your business is becoming much less reliant on you." I said, "I get that; however, my biggest problem is how much tax I have to pay every year."

He said, "You don't have a tax problem; you have a profit problem." This comment annoyed the hell out of me at first, but as if by magic, I had the reason to fix my pricing mindset. I didn't have a tax problem. I had a profit problem. All that self-talk about people won't pay more for landscaping disappeared—it had to. Another 'things to change' moment.

The bigger the tax bill, the bigger the earnings. It wasn't the taxes causing me a problem; it was my lack of discipline in not ring-fencing the money. Owning that feeling was transformative.

Now ownership is a real skill. It's where the rubber meets the road in terms of growth. When you understand you own everything that happens in your life, you have the upper hand. The day the penny dropped was magical. I didn't need to own UP I needed to own IT.

Hmmm…

Own everything

Like most things in life, it's not always our fault.

Could be exposure to someone else's beliefs (parents/teacher/friends); could be a lack of knowledge. We don't know what we don't know. It's not an easy road. If it were, it would be a busy road. And as you know, being a small business owner and entrepreneur is often lonely. You have to figure it out a lot of the time.

So, I do forgive myself for all the mistakes I've made, both professionally and personally. To me, it's one way of owning the past and owning where you are right now. Like I said, you don't know what you don't know.

On the flip side of this is how you own your current circumstances. You know, we're all a victim of our circumstances to some degree, but you can't remain a victim. Being uneducated only acts as an excuse for the outside world. And ownership is all internal.

You can tell me anything you want, but you can't kid yourself. Those thoughts eat away at you when you put your head on the pillow at night. 'You can't kid a kidder,' as the saying goes. Once you find out there's a better way and the opportunity presents itself, you will always live with consequences of rejecting it. There's only so many times you'll believe it *perhaps* wasn't right for you.

Sometimes looking yourself in the eye and accepting your weaknesses is difficult. Especially if you're determined to change. It's easy if you want to pretend there isn't a problem. It's also far too easy to fall into the trap of 'owning up' to your weaknesses, which tends to result in you beating yourself up continuously for not being good enough, even though you had no idea what 'good' looked like when you started.

So, yeah, owning up is powerful, but it's not about owning up to your circumstances. You got to where you are now with the knowledge you had. The fact you could have made it easier or could have done things differently isn't worth torturing yourself over.

But now you know, you have to own it. You have to own everything in your business and life.

Poor relationship with your partner? Yes, you have to own that.

Low bank balance and debt? Yes, you have to own that.

Overworked and underpaid? Yes, you have to own that.

Business too reliant on you? Yes, yes, more yesses… it's all yours to own.

Either you own it, or it owns you. You can't bitch, whine, and expect sympathy, because when you look up for it, it won't be there. If anything, the vultures will be circling ready to pick the bones of what you have. In a year's time, you could be a year better, a year wiser, and a year stronger… or you could just be a year older and handling the same problems you have now. The choice really is yours.

Where else in your life do you give so little but expect so much in return?

Own everything that happens because of you (not *to* you; *because* of you) from this day forward, and you'll see change you didn't think possible. No one is going to save you. You need to save yourself.

Starting with the lessons you've learned so far.

The biggest one is: You need to start paying yourself first. Self-care is important, and you deserve to have the finer things in life. Don't ever feel guilty for that.

Time is your biggest asset, and there's only one of you, so value your time more. The value you bring to your customers, your employees, and your suppliers needs appreciation.

It doesn't matter what you've been led to believe in the past, you can change today when you're ready to. How different would life be if you paid yourself what you deserved, and paid it first?

Take control of your life and finances, and own it; do not allow this business to continue without you getting more. When you do, you'll see the whole world through a new set of eyes.

Be happy for others and share your successes with people. You'll inspire the right ones. They'll watch you step up to the plate and be inspired to do the same thing. Remember, if I can do it, you can too.

When you value yourself and everything you bring to the business, you'll attract the people you deserve. Birds of a feather flock together. When your ideal prospect sees you being successful, they feel a magnetic attraction to you.

You're so close to being, doing, and having everything you want in life. Be brave enough to take the next step. From my story, you'll know I've walked in your shoes, and I'm telling you, all the things you want are in front of you.

The decision you know you must make, the person you know you have to hire, the time you need to spend with someone.

Summary

Where we grow up does have a detrimental effect on our beliefs about money, especially our self-worth. Knowing this gives you power because you can change it.

What we earn isn't as much of an issue as what we do with what we earn. If you make your money work harder for you, you'll begin to eliminate anxieties about the future. Simple saving plans still work.

Nothing beats having control over your finances; otherwise, they control you. When you take charge and pay yourself first, you reap the rewards. And it's ok to be successful and share it with people because it inspires them —and that's not bragging.

What you have, or don't have, is down to you, so own it and start today to change it.

Lesson 2

Most business owners try to do all their accounts themselves—don't!

When you're ready to understand what accounting for your business is about, head over to www.barryrandall.co.uk/booklessons and watch my video: **why you should stop doing your accounting yourself...**

3

WHAT DO YOU WANT TO BE?

How to Use Positioning and Branding to Increase Your Profits

 Your brand is what people say about you when you're not in the room.
~ Jeff Bezos

No more kidding yourself about who you are and who you want to be. You got here by accident, but now the excuses stop. There's no more trial and error. There's no more suck it and see.

It's decision time.

Do you actually want to make more money?

Do you actually want to value yourself more highly?

Then stop giving it away. What's it going to be?

Because you can't build a business that serves everyone. When you're chasing two targets, you miss both. A man who chases two rabbits catches none. So, who is it going to be? What customers do you want? The ones who pay the most is the usual reply I get to this question, but those customers also expect a lot. Is your business set up for this level of customer?

Think about your best ever customer. What is it about

them that makes them the best? Do you want more of them? Was the work profitable or enjoyable? There's so much to consider when you grow your business. Are you starting to see why it hasn't yet happened for you? All of these things are going on around you, and you're doing something else in your business.

If I simplify this and look at two completely different target markets, it might help you to understand it a little more. Take Primark, for example. What kind of customers is Primark targeting, and what type of customers use Primark?

Then take John Lewis as the next example. What kind of customers are they targeting, and what type of customers use John Lewis?

Are they a little different, or completely different? Of course, they're nothing alike—they're chalk and cheese. Which means the marketing messages are different, too. The look of the store is different. The way they train their staff is different. How the staff treat the customers is different.

I'll give you one more example to demonstrate the point before you go off and decide what type of business you want to become and what kind of customers you want to serve. Have you ever been to a B&B at the seaside (doesn't have to be the seaside, you get my point)? The parking spaces are usually tight (if there are any), the décor usually needs updating, the owners usually run the place. You'll also notice they don't follow scripts, and call you by your name, or mate, darling, pal. There's a slight lack of organisation. A bit like they're shocked to see you.

Now, this isn't a dig at B&Bs—I've had some amazing stays in B&Bs over the years, and I know some of them are at the top of their game, but compare a B&B to a five-star hotel. Have you ever been to a five-star hotel? When you arrive, it has valet parking, and the staff wears suits better than the one I wore for my wedding. The décor is immaculate. Crystal chandeliers and shiny surfaces. The staff follows scripts to the letter; they call you sir and madam. They know exactly where your room is, and have your bags carried to the room for you. The experience is completely different.

None of that is an accident. It's all designed that way to attract the right level of customer. Does it cost a whole heap more to stay in a five-star hotel? Absolutely, it does. And here's the thing; people will pay for that level of service. If you're not attracting the right group of customers, maybe you don't have the right level of service for them. Your world-class landscaping skills won't attract high paying customers. But your world-class service will.

I thought price drove all decision making; how wrong I was.

Price is what you pay—value is what you get

Why would people pay more money (in a lot of cases) for a lower level of skill? Because most customers wouldn't know a world-class landscaper from an average landscaper. Because they don't know how to do landscaping. What people do value is the effort you put into the project. The communication skills. The attention to detail in paperwork. The way you look and talk. All those things you put secondary to landscaping.

Why do people pay £500 a night in a five-star hotel, and others only want to pay £50 a night in a B&B? It depends on what you see as value. You and I both know a customer can get a cheaper job done by an equally skilled landscaper, but they choose you. Why? Perceived value. Something you do is valued more than the cheaper price.

Price is the number you give them; value is the feeling you leave them with. Everybody will pay more if they think they'll get a better job, and what that means is a better service. What's going on in a customer's mind before they say yes or no?

- Can I trust you?
- Will you be reliable?
- Does this feel right?
- What if you get it wrong?

None of what goes through their mind ever focuses on the landscaping or the thing they're buying. It's always around reliability, trust, service, and respect.

That's why a great marketer with average landscaping skills wins more work than a great landscaper with average marketing skills. Hands down, every day. If I do my research, understand your audience, and take away my assumptions, I can walk into your local area and appropriate all the clients. Simply by knowing what they want and are prepared to invest in.

What your customers want, need, and pay for

I judge, you judge, we all judge in a nanosecond. The minute you see someone, you're mentally scanning them and working out their background, likely net worth, and anything else that you deem important to know.

In sales meetings, when we rock up at a prospect's place, we often decide before we meet them if they have enough disposable income to buy what we're selling. That's not unusual. It happens every day. Assumptive selling is how you make your fortune, but everyone I train in sales has a problem with assumptions—they make the wrong ones.

I won't go too deep on the selling assumptions. I just want to highlight the things holding you back and possibly creating the bottlenecks in your business. You just need to remove the most unhelpful two words you can use in any conversation:

'I think…'

'I think' is your assumption, and 'I think this prospect is wasting our time' is your excuse. I've spent hundreds of hours training hapless salespeople who are assuming wrongly. You should always assume the prospect wants what you're selling; otherwise, you wouldn't be sitting in front of them. If they didn't want what you were presenting, why would they invite you in?

How do we know they can't afford it? Have we listened to them? Have we understood their wants and desires? Don't make assumptions about something until you've asked all the questions and listened 'properly' to all the answers. And remove 'I think' from your decision-making. If your assumptions are wrong, you'll be fearing rejection and not looking forward to the conversation. That's why you make a positive assumption, then every conversation becomes straightforward.

It's so easy to lose a prospect by assuming they want to spend less money and making a suggestion before you've understood the real reason for the meeting.

I'll finish up by assuming you're going to take this on board and never make any assumptions about pricing again. If the client won't pay it, move on. Never waste energy thinking about what they could or couldn't say about the price. And don't be surprised when someone pays you twice as much as you're charging now, simply by knowing what they want. It's happened to many people just like you.

No surprises in sales

In sales, you never want to surprise anyone—unless it's a good surprise. You should have a set price for the work you do and never move from that number, despite what a prospect tells you in your sales meetings. The notion of landscaping having a fixed rate is nonsense.

I have clients who charge £720 per person per day and others who charge £500 per person per day. And, yes, they have more work than they can manage. Price is something unique to your business and the lifestyle you want your business to produce for you. If you're having difficulty achieving the prices you want, you need to up your sales knowledge and skills.

I've spent hours producing training videos and strategies for all manner of sales situations, which I've got included in our high-level Black Diamond mentoring program here: www.landscaperssuccessclub.com/discover.

In the group, we've got a whole bunch of landscapers turned salespeople. It's inspiring to watch the change in them once they get to grips with the process. We all get in a bubble of pricing at an amount we believe a client will pay rather than an amount we want them to pay. Don't second guess the client's budget, just decide your worth in numbers and stick to it.

Whatever you're charging now, I believe it's possible to double it. That's without knowing the number. I haven't met a landscaper yet who couldn't double their prices. And we have landscapers in England, Ireland, Scotland, and Wales. This system works for anyone who applies it and is willing to make the changes needed to become a better business owner.

Think about it. Do you make enough money for all the hard work you put into the business? Are you working harder than you thought you would have to? Do your family see the best of you when you get home? All these things start with knowing your true value as a person. Forget the business for a second, because none of this is about a profitable business. It's about a confident person who has high self-worth.

You should never feel guilty for wanting more in life. If you already know you'd be prepared to do anything to make sure the client gets a fantastic job, you should be confident enough to charge for that level of service. If you don't have the confidence, we do. And that is what I'm offering you; a chance to stop doing things the old way and start doing them the right way.

This is not a sales pitch; it's a plea for you to finally open your eyes and see YOU are the one person in this equation who can change everything, just by making the decision.

Today.

Refuse to produce work at the old prices, and never offer discounts.

Never offer discounts without a reason

The bargain hunters smell blood when they see a discount sign. So, it's complete madness. That's what discounting is. Most people don't make enough profit at full price, never mind after discounting. It's usually an attempt to market their business when the work has run out (which takes us back to being consistent, although I want to stay on topic with discounting). Discounting is what I'm aiming to convince you to stop doing.

First of all, if you HAVE to discount, never do it without a reason. You can't go and advertise 10% off your prices when a customer has just paid you the full price. It's a sure way to lose any future recommendations and sends out a warning to high-end clients that you're short of work, or unorganised. Discounts attract all the bargain hunters who then knock the price down even more. Instead of offering 10% off, offer 10% more in value.

Let me explain this very briefly.

If you've quoted £10,000 for a job and you're offering a 10% discount, you're giving away £1,000, which is pure profit assuming you make 10% or more on your projects. Instead of giving away £1,000, it would be better to offer something with a perceived value of £1,000, which costs you less.

For example:

Free pressure washing worth £1,097.

The pressure washing is probably only going to cost you a day in labour for someone, but to the prospect, they're getting £1,000 worth of extras for free. Pressure washing is one example; it could be a plant design, or a pergola, or painting the fence. Anything that makes your proposal more appealing to the prospect.

It's a much better strategy than conditioning your audience to wait because there'll be a discount next week. People are always watching, whether you think they are or not.

Use some of your downtime to work out all the various things you could offer for the same perceived value as a discount, then use some of it to lead your marketing efforts. Whatever you do, don't discount unless you have a very good reason to. It cheapens the product and service you provide. I learned a big lesson in the quote, "Pay cheap pay twice."

Are you too cheap to be this good?

Everyone has a problem with being undercut on price. There's almost always a cheaper alternative with any product or service, but that's not the reason you aren't selling enough. Even if you charged the absolute minimum amount—to the point you were barely scraping by—there'd be someone who could do it for less. And often much less.

If you have the best prices possible on materials and you don't charge any markup on them, there'll still be someone who can find a much cheaper way around the project. It's impossible to compete at the bottom of the barrel. You end up being like a crab in a bucket; everyone climbing on top of each other to get out of the damn thing.

Why would everyone be trying to get out of that market? Because in the one above it, the prices are higher. But what makes them higher? The level of clients you're dealing with. Exactly. The clients you want to be working for are paying higher prices—right? They know it's worth investing a little more (sometimes a lot more) to get the right company.

If you completely agree there's a higher level of client who wants to pay more—because they want certainty, they'll get a better job—how do you know when you've got one of these clients in front of you?

The size of the house?

The car on the drive?

Nope, it's none of those things. Ok, they could be good indicators, but remember what I said before about assumptions; they just make the sale more difficult. The best way to get out of the race to the bottom of the business barrel when you keep getting undercut on price is to increase your prices, not reduce them.

If you find yourself in a battle with another competitor on price, it means the ones you didn't get were because you were too cheap. Then you confirmed the prospect's fears about the price being too low by not following up properly. In landscaping and other trades, the prospect doesn't want to know you can do the job (we all talk too much technical jargon, but I won't go into that here). The prospect knows you can do the job, they researched you and called you after doing that research. What they care about now is how much you want the job.

Start showing your prospects how much you want to do business. You can tell them all about your medals, your awards, your years in business, and how many projects you've built, but if you don't follow up with them and tell them how much you want the work… you're back in the bucket feeding off scraps.

Take this bit of advice and never look back. Increase your communication with the prospect and add 25% to your prices, and you'll be a whole new business in six months. The right people don't want a cheap job. In fact, I once lost a £150,000 project because the client had in mind a price for a little over £200,000 and felt, although we were very professional, we may have missed something on the quote.

It might feel like you're taking a risk increasing your prices by 10%, but clients are risking 100% by getting it wrong. There's a lot at stake for them.

High stakes

Over the last couple of years, I've helped business owners in all different niches totally transform their outlook on business, increase their happiness in their personal life, and essentially build a better business. Occasionally a business comes along, and I end up being a bigger part of it. Sometimes being a mentor is great, but like you, I want to build my own empire as well.

So much can happen if you get the right people looking at your business. And sometimes, just sometimes, you'll find the best opportunity is inside your current business.

Knowledge is power. The sad reality is, most people are intelligent enough to know they need to change; to know if they keep repeating the same things over and over again, they'll get the same results. Yet, they still do. I also believe they're intelligent enough not to ignore the opportunities they find themselves in front of and reading, but I know why they do.

Fear of failure. What if it doesn't work out? The first question we ask ourselves when faced with a life-changing opportunity. Not, 'This is everything I've ever wanted where do I sign up?' but 'What if it doesn't work out?' I was the same. I said the same things. But I was desperate and had no choice. Maybe that's what it takes. Some people can see the pain coming. Some people don't ever want to see the pain coming. Others, like me, need to feel the hurt from the pain before we can change.

Remember, your external transformation (more money, better life, holidays, cars, houses) starts with an internal shift. The day you wake up and say, "That's it, I'm grabbing this opportunity!" That's the only real gamble you have to take. After that moment, you suddenly see everything completely differently. It's as if there's this whole world happening around you, and you can't see it.

Then you find yourself on the other side where all the successful people are, and you're looking at the world you were living in and wondering why those people don't just change their thinking. I can't think of a better way to describe the feeling of empowerment you get from finally fighting resistance to change and just saying, that's it, I'm going in, and I'm going to get what everyone else has.

You have to decide right now whether you want to make money and who you want to serve. You can't give five-star service charging two-star prices... and you'll never do enough for the wrong customer.

Remember, it's not the cost that attracts clients; it's the service and value you bring. Because what customers want, and need are two distinctly different things. And with no off-the-shelf prices in landscaping, you can charge what you want to.

If you're losing jobs to competitors, maybe you're too cheap, not too expensive. So, don't discount, be consistent, and definitely no surprises when you're selling.

Summary

You have to decide right now whether you want to make money and who you want to serve. You can't give five-star service charging two-star prices… and you'll never do enough for the wrong customer.

Remember, it's not the cost that attracts clients; it's the service and value you bring. Because what customers want and need are two distinctly different things. And with no off-the-shelf prices in landscaping, you can charge what you want to.

If you're losing jobs to competitors, maybe you're too

cheap, not too expensive. So, don't discount, be consistent, and definitely no surprises when you're selling.

Lesson 3

Decide who your target is, and increase your prices by 10%. When you're ready to do both of those things, head over to www.barryrandall.co.uk/booklessons and watch my video: **find your target and increase your prices...**

4

WHAT IS MARKETING?

You're Not a Landscaping Business; You're a Marketing Business

 People do not buy goods or services. They buy relations, stories and magic.
~ Seth Godin

In year one of running my business properly, I did a turnover of £377,000 and made a respectable £106,000 in profit. Last year it was close to £300,000 every month with close to £50,000 a month in profit. It all changed when I introduced a marketing system into my business. It started with a simple, but bold, guarantee, and by the end of the first year, I was doing over £50,000 per month revenue. Before the guarantee, I was doing about £8,000 per month.

If I showed you a way to put £50 notes into a pot and pull out £1,000, wouldn't you keep filling the pot with £50 notes? To be honest, you would be utterly unsalvageable if you said no! Well, that's exactly what real marketing is. It was this same philosophy that allowed me to transform my £8,000 into £300,000. I was buying customers, and that makes marketing essential, not expensive.

I know marketing is scary for everyone who isn't a marketing expert, so in this chapter, I'm going to help you get the basics sorted in a non-scary way. In 2012, I was reluctantly paying £90 per month on an advert in the local magazine, and today I comfortably 'enjoy' spending £20,000 a month on advertising with Google and Facebook.

Luckily for you, I'm not going to talk too much about paying a lot of money to get clients; this is more about busting the myths, showing you the traps, and making sure you maximise every opportunity you're currently missing. The biggest marketing myth of them all is… it's a cost. That's just not true. If you do your marketing correctly, it's 100% investment. The great thing for you is, even if you do it poorly, you can often still get a return on the investment. But we'll stick with doing it right.

Remember, everything you do in your business is marketing. The way you speak to clients, the cleanliness of your site, the tidiness of your vehicle. In one way or another, you're always marketing yourself. So, bear that in mind when you look at the rubbish in your windows, or on the passenger seat. How you do something is how you do everything. Clients see it, even if you don't.

You also have to be able to switch it up and down when you need to. Word-of-mouth, for example, isn't a marketing strategy in and of itself; it's not scalable. It can keep you busy at times, but you can't get more word-of-mouth when YOU want it. It happens organically.

Throughout this chapter, I'm going to give you some simple tips to improve your lead generation without going to the bank for a working capital loan. And you won't need a degree in marketing to do what I'll teach you.

Fortunately for you (and I), I'm part of an elite marketing mastermind group in the USA, so I've busted all the myths wide open and created marketing machines for hundreds of businesses. And in this chapter, I'm revealing some implementable ideas that will double the number of leads you get.

Things like:

- Asking for referrals
- Why it's important to communicate regularly
- Why word-of-mouth could be ruining your business
- Why doing an amazing job isn't enough anymore
- Why most advertisers can't measure results
- How to get Google reviews

I'll let you into a secret… it's not how often you advertise, but where you advertise. Where there's one great customer, there's usually a whole bunch more.

Birds of a feather flock together

Ralph Waldo Emerson once, famously, said, "Build a better mousetrap and the world will beat a path to your door." Notice he didn't say build a 'different' mousetrap. Really crucial bit of information. And as marketing is about the small details, this one stands out the most.

You see, marketing is pretty elementary at a high level. You simply need to know who your target it is, how your target buys, and where your target is. Then convince your targets to buy from you. Which is why target market researching is the number one most important thing you can get right for your business.

I'm going to guess you have a wide range of customers you service. Different age ranges, different income brackets, different requirements and tastes… which means you're getting enquiries by accident. Or more succinctly, your customers found you, rather than you finding them.

Maybe at this point, you didn't know you could locate, attract, and convert your ideal prospect into a customer. But you do now, so time to own it. To keep what could get complicated very, very simple, I want you to take a couple of seconds to think about the best customer you ever worked for. The name should jump out at you reasonably swiftly.

- What was the person's name?
- Where did they live?
- Age?
- Backstory?
- Hobbies?
- What car did they drive?

This information forms a client avatar, which you use to develop your marketing efforts. Now you've got this customer in mind, do you think there are more like them around? Enough to fill your diary? I'll give you the straightforward answer—yes, there are.

Now you know who it is, what car they drive, and what hobbies they have, you know exactly where to find them. If they play golf—amazing, I wonder if the club where they're a member has a yearly presentation you could sponsor? If they drive a BMW—amazing, I wonder what would happen if you had a BMW in your advertising picture?

Again, these things are simple when you know how. It's the thinking that's hard work. There's no instant gratification in sitting down and thinking about your ideal client, but the result is worth it when you do. Then it's a simple exercise in economics. Once you've found one ideal client, you'll know where the others are; remember, birds of a feather flock together.

Amaze one, and the rest will beat a path to your door. You just have a decision to make on your door. Is it a shop front, somewhere people can visit and speak to you? Or is your door more impersonal, like a website?

Choosing a website as a door can be costly if you don't understand where your target market is. It doesn't have to be, because you don't need an all-singing, all-dancing website to get great results—you can start small and then build a bigger door.

You don't need a new website

I want to reassure you that you won't need to invest £25,000 on a new website to attract the best clients. Absolutely, a well-designed, easy to navigate website is going to help you get better clients, but you can't go from no website to an all-singing, all-dancing website immediately—nor do you need to.

Here's what you need from a website to attract the right clients…

Number one, you need it to load promptly. The worst thing you could have is a fancy website that loads slowly when prospects click on the link—they'll bounce away and never be seen again (unless you used paid traffic, which we'll touch on at the end of this chapter).

You need a sound home page with a striking headline at the top, a great image of a finished garden beneath the headline, and a call to action under the image. Those are the first things your website visitor should see. Not your logo and company name—no one cares about those things when they're looking for a new garden.

If you don't have any skilfully taken images of your finished work, I suggest you pick up a camera or hire a professional photographer to go and take a few pictures for you. You don't need hundreds of images, just a handful to use on your website that showcase the work to people who visit and want to know more about the company.

Photos don't need to feature your latest project, because the garden you did last year is still new to a first-time visitor. Remember, if you've decided who your target market is, you'll want to use pictures of projects that are likely to attract the right prospects. People buy what they see and what they read. So, you'd do well to remember a picture may well speak a thousand words; just make sure it's not the wrong words. I'll come to the call to action in a separate chapter.

A suitable home page, a solid About Us page, a portfolio or gallery page, a blog page, and a contact page are great (I'll cover adding pages later). Those five pages will be more than enough to get you in front of the right prospects, and the right words and images will influence them to call. You can pay cheap, but you may be paying twice, so listen to people who are suggesting anywhere between £1,500 and £2,500 for the website.

Don't make the mistake of being too technical on your website. Remember, your average prospect has no knowledge of landscaping or garden design, so using jargon won't impress them—it will put them off. It's much better to explain the process they go through (in layman's terms) than to overload them with information on how you do landscaping. At this stage, they only want to know what's next; you can explain the technical stuff down the track.

You might think of 'user-friendly' as a term relating to people who aren't good at using computers, but think back to the last time you tried to buy something you weren't sure about—it would have been a challenge. User-friendly is all about the experience visitors have on your website, not how easy it is to use. After all, how much easier do you need it to be than clicking a few buttons?

Navigate people through the site: 'Now visit our contact page and leave us a short message, and we'll do all the work for you.' On the contact page, make sure you spell out what you want visitors to do—don't assume they know just because you do.

Instead of 'Complete your contact details and we'll call you back.' Why not say, 'Tell us what you're most unsure about, and we'll send you some information to make it clearer for you before we talk.' Keep it simple. Attract them in. Ask for something small, like an email address.

The only purpose of your website...

...is to collect email addresses. I heard this at a super conference in Jacksonville, Florida. It intrigued me. Up until then, an email address was a way of communicating with someone I was working with, or for. I hadn't heard of, let alone understood, the power of email marketing.

There are hundreds of different email marketing software products you can use to automate your delivery. This article gives you the best nine:

www.isitwp.com/best-email-marketing-services-compared

Email marketing is still so powerful for communication. Mainly because you can reach all your prospects, and customers, at the same time, by sending one email. You can even see if any of them have opened the email or not.

This strategy is powerful with five to ten email

addresses, so when you have 15,000, you have an opportunity to sell to all of them at the same time. Imagine that. You can send the same message to everyone who has expressed interest in your business at once. It's like putting a salesperson in front of each of your 15,000 prospects.

When you add this to having a list of your ideal targets, it means you're using the language they all understand on the email, so the email feels and sounds completely personal to them.

From today, start collecting emails from prospects and customers and begin sending weekly messages. On one list you should have all your customers, and each week you send them some news or information about the business. On the other list, you send them an email each week selling your services to them.

Your customers will be grateful for the constant contact —in fact, most will forget you if you don't stay in touch. The prospects have a constant reminder you're there, so they don't make a decision without including you in it.

An email each week for each of the lists should take you no more than 30 minutes. If you're stretched for time, you could outsource those emails for £10-£15 per week. The return you get will be worth every penny.

It's much more scalable than word-of-mouth, which can often attract the wrong customers.

All my work comes from word-of-mouth

"My work speaks for itself." "I get all my work by word-of-mouth." I've heard these comments far too many times in the landscaping industry, and the conversations never end well. Mainly because people aren't sure what the comments mean. Earlier I said word-of-mouth isn't a scalable marketing strategy, (which it isn't), but it's also a poor advert for your business if you don't know what people are really saying about you.

And I can't imagine you've ever stopped to ask the question. I mean, why would you? As long as the work keeps coming in, you must be doing something right. Plus, referrals are the easiest work to sell. Usually, they say yes before you've even gone to meet them, based purely on word-of-mouth. But there's a big difference between a referral and word-of-mouth. I'll explain later.

The problem with word-of-mouth business is the clients all say too much. So, not only have you got the job before you see it, but they've also got the price before you show it. That's the downside of word-of-mouth. And word-of-mouth never sounds like this:

"Hey, John, you should use my landscaper. He's methodical, takes his time, everything's immaculate, and he uses all the best materials. By the way, sit down when he tells you the price because he's bloody expensive. Worth every penny, but expensive."

It just doesn't happen like that. It's more like:

"Hey, John, why don't you get your garden done? My landscaper is looking for some more work. He's cheap as chips, does a good job, and I'll be able to have a word and get you a good deal because you're my friend. Oh, by the way, if you push him, he'll bring his price down a bit."

Do you understand where I'm coming from with this word-of-mouth thing? To me, word-of-mouth is a bit of a marketing trap. You get stuck doing jobs at a price that suits the client, not you. And because you have a relationship with the person who passed on your details, you can be pulled emotionally to do someone a favour.

I'm not saying this is necessarily you, but it happens to a lot of great tradespeople. So, of all the marketing scams, pitfalls, and traps, this is one you want to avoid. Make sure what people say about you is serving you well for the future. Being great value, honest, and doing a fine job is not good word-of-mouth. Being expensive but worth it—is.

When you have the right people saying the right things, it's time to scale and implement a sound, reliable referral system.

Increase referrals overnight with this one single tip

Referrals are a different animal altogether from word-of-mouth. If you get the right referral system in place, it can scale your business as fast as you can keep control of it. There's one terrific referral strategy that works every time and won't cost you much at all to implement immediately, starting from the end of this marketing chapter.

But before I reveal the strategy, you must see these types of promotions all the time, so there are lots to model from. 'Refer a friend and get dinner on us.' 'Refer a friend, and you both get 50% off your next haircut.' You don't need to reinvent the wheel. If it works, it works. I would lean towards the referrals where both parties gain. They're typically easier to sell to clients, simply because a referral can feel like you're persuading someone to buy something, and if they're gaining from it, they feel uneasy about it. But if the person they're referring to is going to gain as well, it's an easier decision.

I've tried many different referral strategies along the way:

- £100 garden centre voucher
- £50 John Lewis voucher
- A luxury hamper for two
- Tickets to RHS Chelsea
- A luxury hotel stay

- A gas BBQ and wine cooler
- A Lay-Z-Spa® hot tub

These are just a few examples of incentives I've tried and succeeded with. But none work as well as our current strategy. The one that most people often neglect to use because they can't think of an appropriate gift.

I'll keep this genuinely simple.

When you finish the project, take a handful of referral cards to your customer and say this one line: "If you're happy with the service we provided, would you please recommend me to your friends and family."

Yeah, just ask, and ask frequently. Send referral cards out in the post every month if you have to. You can offer the best gift in the world, but it's meaningless unless you ask for referrals.

If I could leave you with a tip for getting more referrals, it would be to create a process where your customer hands a friend a referral card and writes their name on it. When the prospect calls and tells you their friend referred you, send them both a thank-you card with a £10 Amazon voucher inside—whether you get the job or not.

Reward the effort, not the result. It gives the prospect a story to tell, and who doesn't like hearing a good, positive story about being treated well?

The power of storytelling

With a sound target in your sights and a clear understanding of your prospective clients' interests and aspirations, you can start writing copy that talks directly to them. Once again, leave the technical terms for the landscapers.

Write clear messages in all your adverts, social media posts, and email copy. If your target is a 60-year-old semi-retired golf player, use language like, 'A New Lawn As Flat As a Putting Green,' because the more specific you are in your communications—especially in your copy—the more you can draw out your perfect prospect.

Don't concern yourself with the people who don't get drawn out. You can't attract everyone. You could get even more targeted and lead with, 'Are You a Semi-Retired Golf Lover Looking For a New Garden?' The thing to remember when doing your website and email copy is to focus on your target and eliminate the rest. You'll still get some people who don't fall into your ideal customer profile, which isn't a problem—you can take those prospects through your sales funnel. The aim isn't to eliminate everyone; it's to draw out the right people.

Once they raise their hand and express interest, you'll have to convert them into customers. Why would they choose you over and above any of your competition? What makes you the correct choice? It's not uniformed staff and comprehensive insurance cover. Of course, they help, but what a prospect most wants to know is; what do I get if I become a customer… and what do I lose if I don't?

Your copy has to walk them through… and then in. The more you can talk to what a prospect wants, the better. None of them is looking for a landscaper whose website homepage says they're insured and have a fleet of vehicles. They're looking for one simple thing: If I call this person, will I get **exactly** what I want?

One of the best ways to keep people reading is to use stories. You can use stories about past customer projects, or case studies from delighted customers—both are great ways of showing social proof and building upfront confidence before they call you.

Remember, just because you know you're a reputable, reliable, and skilled craftsperson doesn't mean they do. Just because you tell them you've got hundreds of delighted clients, doesn't mean you have. That's why client case studies are so powerful, yet so neglected. I'll come to that soon.

You need to present people with all the evidence upfront to call you, not rely on getting in front of them— because you might not get the opportunity if you handle this bit wrong. Pull on those emotional levers. Make sure you read through the testimonial section of this chapter because it'll talk you through how to get the right case studies in place for every step of the process.

To demonstrate my point; when you first picked up this book, you may have been a bit sceptical about the author (me). Slowly, throughout the book, I've demonstrated through stories that I'm someone you can trust. Because what I'm telling you isn't theoretical, it's not just a paper exercise; it's actually a real-life business owner, who has gone through the same challenges you're having, and he has evidence to back it all up.

In the client success stories section, I've listed a handful of testimonials I've received from clients who've had huge turnarounds in their businesses and personal lives working alongside me. Each one of them I'm proud of, and I want you to see how much communication and storytelling matters in writing and written communication.

Use storytelling in all your communication:

- Web copy
- Ad copy
- Emails
- Proposals
- Quotes

- Text messages

Each one is equally important, and it's essential to get them right when you're trying to locate, attract, and convert prospects into customers, then eventually into advocates—clients who refer you on to friends and family members.

Most people don't know how to introduce you. Just saying 'Barry did a great job' is ok, but ok strategies get ok results. Everyone is silently begging to be led… so, lead them, and teach them how to get you more business.

Not everyone takes action

The biggest crime in marketing is to finish an email, a social media post, or a letter without a call to action. It drives me insane when I see people do it (and I sometimes have to pull my team up on it!)

But what is a call to action or CTA? Good question. It's the part of a web page, advert, or email content that encourages the person reading it to do something—take action. Hence the name. On your website, a CTA might be to 'Enquire here,' or 'Download our free guide.' In an email, it could be 'Call us to book your start date.' In an advert, it might be 'For more information, email us.'

Your CTA drives a variety of different actions depending on the objective of the marketing campaign. Again, it all comes back to your target and what you want them to do when they see your advert, which is why it's important to remember everyone is silently begging for someone to lead them. When you finish a post or email without demanding someone take some sort of action, they often feel unfulfilled. Which usually means lost £££s.

The actions taken by readers form the data you'll use

for testing and measuring to build your future sales as you grow your business. If there's no action taken, the marketing often gets dismissed as not working; but if you don't tell them what to do, they won't do it. How can they? If *you* aren't sure what you want them to do, they must have zero idea.

And use power words like NOW and TODAY. For example, instead of saying 'Call us on 0116 2100 777,' say 'Call us NOW on 0116 2100 777.' To you, it may seem like being pushy, but to a reader, it's giving direction.

To get some quick wins, go onto your Facebook page and add CTAs to your last ten posts. It might not have an immediate impact, but it sets a standard for you to follow from now on in.

The results of your tests could form future marketing decisions. Testing allows you to fail, which, by the way, is ok. The idea of testing is to eliminate all the CTAs that won't encourage people to contact you. Typically, I would ask clients to write five to ten CTAs and test them all.

Give it a try. Write five calls to action for your business and test them on your latest social media posts.

Not everything works

Advertising without testing and measuring is the equivalent of winding your vehicle's window down in the morning and throwing a bunch of cash out onto the motorway.

Especially when you consider it's likely that 80% of your first efforts won't work. The idea is to test (or try) a new idea and then measure the results you get before you turn it up and run it more aggressively. I'll give you a couple of examples to run with.

A company approaches you to advertise in their magazines. They have a distribution of 20,000 homes locally. Number one, how many of those homes have your target clients in them? Number two, just because the targets live in those areas doesn't mean they'll read your ad. Before you agree to go in all the magazines, test an advert in one magazine and record the results by asking the people who enquire where they got your number from. At the end of the month, you look at the results and see if you've had a favourable return on your investment.

For demonstration purposes, let's say the advert cost you £100 and you received two phone calls. That means your cost to get an enquiry is £50. If you sold one of those projects for £3,000, your marketing cost to get the job would be £100.

Armed with those stats from your testing and measuring, you can now go into the second magazine. Only this time, you run the first advert in the first magazine again and run the same advert with a different headline in the second magazine. At the end of the month, you measure the results from each magazine. If advert two in magazine two had a better result, you run the winning advert in both magazines.

You could keep changing headlines, calls to action, and images on the adverts to improve your results month on month, which is why testing and measuring is so crucial to your marketing spend.

Another example is doing a leaflet drop. I know it's cheaper per leaflet to print 10,000 than it is to print 100, but before you go to the expense and time of printing and delivering 10,000, you need to know what the return is on a hundred. Great marketing takes time, patience, and insightful analysis. Plus, you should only change one thing at a time. If you change more than one thing, you won't know which bit got you the improved results.

Test and measure everything in your business. Record

the performance of all your marketing efforts. How many people call in? How many become customers? How much did it cost to acquire that customer? If you reflect on the advert example of getting one £3,000 project from a £100 ad spend, you now know that for every £1 you spend, you get £30 in return (in that particular magazine).

All your marketing will achieve different results, but ultimately when you have it up and running, you should get a return on your investment for every pound you spend. Over time, I've got my marketing spend to be anywhere between 5% and 7% of my monthly revenue. That's why I'm comfortable investing £20,000 per month into paid traffic, because it's only 7% of what the business produces in revenue.

This part of the book isn't about designing massively sophisticated marketing strategies—it aims to give you confidence so you can keep getting new enquiries with the right marketing. So, the takeaway from this is to go and ask every prospect who calls where they found your number. If you have advertising running, you'll be able to see how effective it is. If you don't record where your calls are coming from, you might be wasting money on advertising that isn't working.

Once you have that information and you know where your audience is, you can design the advert to put in front of them and gather reviews that speak directly to them. Because what other people say about you is gospel; what you say about yourself is bragging. Don't take my word for it.

The immense power of client testimonials

If you aim for a satisfied client, the best you can ever get is satisfied clients. If you aim for a delighted client...

At any stage of business, we all understand, you're only as good as your last job. Not because you say so, but because the customer says so, which means client testimonials and stories (what they tell people about you when you're not there) build your reputation. But it's no good having lots of delighted clients if no one else knows about it. You'd be surprised how helpful a positive review on Google from a happy client can be when closing a big deal.

From today onwards, you need to use client testimonials as a strategy, not when they give you a review. By that, I simply mean you must get a review from every one of your clients. Not only do they assist your sales, but they also give you great feedback to build on or learn from.

I can hear you thinking, how do I get them all to give me a review, write a testimonial or go in front of a camera? Easy. A nice ethical bribe will do you the world of good. A £10 Amazon voucher is an excellent gift to send for a review, and it's obviously worth a lot more than £10 to you as a business to get a good, solid review you can use on your website or social media.

Back to how to get the review. When you finish a project, before you collect the final balance, send out or leave a questionnaire for the client to complete. Nothing too taxing, just a simple set of questions with three optional answers. I suggest ten questions are more than enough and only take a few minutes to complete.

If you ask before the final bill, you'll get the questionnaire completed. If you ask after the client's paid the final bill, you perhaps won't get it completed, plus it's going to create an administration job to chase them up, anyway.

Here's an example of a typical question:

What would you say best describes our service?

Then give three options. Good, very good, or excellent (you'll notice the options are all positive). Often, if you leave a blank box and ask the client to be creative, you're less likely to get anything back. If it seems like hard work, they won't bother.

Once you have the testimonials, you can weave them into a case study, which is great for landing pages and Facebook ad copy later down the line when the business starts investing in more paid traffic. All of my success club members get the system to create sales converting case studies, even if they only have small bits of feedback from customers.

The right clients can double your business

Around 87% of clients would rather pay someone else to repair faulty work than call you back to correct it—quite scary statistics. I've seen lots of landscapers proudly say they never get any snags. It's virtually impossible to complete a landscaping project without ever having some remedial work to do.

The weather, plant life, just general wear and tear is going to cause problems. So much so, I have a full-time aftercare team to look after any client who has even the smallest problem.

Have you ever been called out to quote for a project where someone has already been and not done a great job? It happens all the time. These are the 87% of clients who would rather pay someone else to fix it than claim on their guarantee. Of course, you get some customers who will never be happy no matter what you do for them. The thing is, you tend to react to those customers and try to do your best for them. To please them.

Generally, it works something like this: 15% of

customers will be on the phone and demanding you repair anything that isn't to their liking, and another 15% will never correct anything that moves. Then there's the 70% in the middle who want something fixing but are a bit intimidated or hesitant, so they never call you.

It's your job as a business owner to make that call easy for them. I appreciate that the less snagging you get, the better because we're all too busy on paid work to be going back to unpaid work. However, snagging is where you build the business. Keep in touch with your past customers and clients. Build a longer-term relationship with them. Make sure you attend to their issues, and you work as hard to impress them after they've given you the work as you did before they gave you the work.

A quick story. I had a builder from a referral networking organisation come to do a garage conversion for me at my home. When he took the job on, he was legitimately short of work. Towards the end of the job, he was getting sloppy and not turning in each day. I found out he'd got a bigger, better job through his referral networking, and my job was now a pain to him.

The project never got finished to my satisfaction, and the builder has never once called to see whether the work is still ok or if I have anyone to recommend to him. As it happens, I've had to have all the electrics redone. All the plastering redone. The flooring is sticking. And he left the driveway in a mess.

This is someone who relies on referrals from his networking group to get more business. Fundamentally, he understands referrals are about building relationships, but in my case, he couldn't build a garage, let alone a relationship!

I understand things do go wrong on projects, and it's our position as business owners to give customers a way of letting us know without them fearing they're an inconvenience to us.

They remember how keen you were to win the work, how nothing was a problem to start with, and that you were always available in the beginning. Make sure clients remember you long after the project is complete. Just go back to the email marketing section on page 77, set up a monthly email list, and send out a note.

Yes, you'll invite some snagging work, but you should welcome it. After all, a good guarantee should guarantee a good business. Plus, if you're charging enough, you won't feel bad about having to complete some snagging work.

You can't beat a good guarantee

My first big, bold guarantee was, 'If you don't love your finished garden, it's free.' It worked like magic for me! At the beginning of this chapter, I told you how in year one of my business I did a turnover of £377,000 and made £106,000 in profit. How all those painful lessons helped build my businesses. Well, looking back and reflecting while writing this, I realise I got so much wrong in that first year, I could easily have doubled the profit with the right knowledge and experience.

I wasn't brand new to working for myself when I started my business. I had already done a few years as a subcontractor, so I had some customers who were providing low-paid work. I met my coach and turned my subcontracting work into a registered business. But that's not enough by itself. Being a registered business isn't going to guarantee your success.

And that's the point. We won't go into anything if we can't guarantee it's going to work and it'll be value for money. Even buying this book needed a certain guarantee for you—a promise it would work. Clients want those same guarantees, especially when they're investing so much money into a project. Often, they've saved for years to have the work done; the last thing they want is for it to go wrong, or if it goes wrong for it to have to be paid for again.

That's where a HUGE promise comes in. A money-back guarantee. A risk reversal. Something so powerful clients will be absolutely sure you're the person they want for the job. If there's a problem, they want to feel confident you'll fix it. For every horror story you've heard, you've also heard the good guy story. Prospects haven't. When people are parting with money, they see horror stories.

SO, my first 'proper' guarantee was:

If you don't love your finished garden, it's free.

Every person I spoke to said it was a crazy idea, that it would attract people who wanted a free garden. They were utterly wrong. That advertisement took me from a tiny little business to £377k worth of revenue in the first year. And I only had one person who tried to use the guarantee to get the work for free.

I went back and changed what they said wasn't right, and they paid up. But here's the thing. By the end of the first year, I was bringing in over £50,000 per month in revenue. Before the guarantee, I was doing about £8,000 per month. I'm not saying you should use the exact same guarantee I did; maybe I was crazy! But think about it for a second; what could you offer as a guarantee to convince clients to buy from you?

I know this for a fact because I carried out the advertising campaign. If you put in a guarantee to pay for the garden if the client's not happy, you will attract some people who are nasty and want to get a free garden. That in itself is enough to put you off trying. But the better way to look at this is; if I put the guarantee in place, I will 100% get more work than I would without it. For me, that was £42,000 per month more—as my average garden was £4,000 then, it means I was getting at least ten more sales a month by using a strong guarantee than I was without one. Let's say my average build was £10,000, and the new guarantee attracted ten more build sales, but once a month someone claimed a free garden (it wouldn't happen but let's say it did). I'd still be doing nine gardens more than I was before having the guarantee.

Business is all about knowing your numbers. Especially in marketing. Buying customers. Lifetime value. Average value. All these things matter. So, next time you're faced with a client saying, "We chose the competitor because it was cheaper," ask yourself, would a solid guarantee have won me this job?

The alternative is missing out on work because you don't have the right offer in place. You're not giving the right certainty, and that makes the winter months a more substantial challenge than they need to be.

More elephant cleaning

Remember when we were thinking about cleaning elephants back in Chapter One as a way of achieving goals by breaking them down into smaller parts? Well, elephants can help with marketing too, because marketing is scary for most business owners, and I understand why. I've had enough people promise me the world and not deliver on their promises. When you see marketing as a massive, scary task, it's often easier to not tackle it at all, which is why I wanted to use the elephant analogy. To eliminate some of the fear, you break it down small piece by small piece.

I recall a time when a local magazine agent—who lives

close to me—came to my office and offered advertising space that was remarkably cheap because he'd had some cancellations. It was in December 2013. I got talking to him and asked why the other people had cancelled. He said, "They ran out of work so couldn't afford to advertise." Fairly typical scenario for most business owners and something I'd done in the not too distant past.

It's crazy though, isn't it? If you run out of work, the last thing you should cut is your advertising. But it's the norm; people always do it. The real question is, how did you get to the point where you ran out of work and money? I know the answer, so it's not really a question; zero consistency in their business. They advertise when they need work, instead of advertising so that they don't need work.

Let me explain. If you're consistent with everything in your business, you'll never have problems with it. Expecting miracles now and again isn't a scalable business strategy—occasionally you get something come along and save you, by luck or divine intervention. But you've heard the saying, 'Fail to prepare, prepare to fail?' It's this.

Most business owners advertise in the summer and have more enquiries than they can handle, so they get careless and spill lots of them. They don't plan for the winter and are then surprised every year when they run out of work, or bad weather means it's impossible to make any money.

Look, I was one of these people, and I realise how bloody stupid it is. It's business suicide. And that's just advertising—I used to do the same with employees. Hire people in the summer, lay them off in the winter, someone else hires them, I'm back to square one. That's the hamster wheel effect we've talked about. Repeating the same pattern each year over and over and getting worse, not better.

At some point, we have to take the risk of becoming a proper business, and it requires consistency—real solid consistency. That's where accountability comes in. Remember the guy who didn't want to be told what to do in his own business? Yeah, him.

If you were him and someone like me was constantly reminding you about the winter coming and worked with you on a plan, you wouldn't have half the trouble you're experiencing this year. Again, this isn't just about work; it's about the weather, team members, staying on top of your receipts.

Consistency beats flashes of genius every day of the week. Just the discipline of showing up every time on time will change the way you run your life and your business.

Summary

You wouldn't ask someone to marry you on the first date, and for good reason. Building a lasting relationship takes time, consistency, and an appreciation for your client's wants and needs.

Marketing is like a good relationship. The more you keep in touch, share stories, and add value, the more likely you are to do business with someone.

Marketing can seem like a big task for any small business owner; however, it's the one thing that takes you from small business to bigger business without the worry of where the work is going to come from.

If you do a great job, offer a great guarantee—and always ask for a review. If you want more customers like your existing ones, get them to find new clients for you.

Lesson 4

Create a strong guarantee and make it front and centre of your marketing.

When you're ready to understand how powerful a guarantee is for your business and why putting one front and centre of your marketing will transform your profits, head over to www.barryrandall.co.uk/booklessons and watch the video: **why a powerful guarantee will get you more business...**

5

THE ART OF COMMUNICATION

How to Charm Employees, Clients, and Suppliers into Working in Harmony

 Wisemen speak because they have something to say. Fools because they have to say something.
~ **Plato**

B asic communication skills and processes can turn your business around and send you off in a completely different direction. You could have the best product and a fantastic team, but poor communication makes you look like amateurs.

In this chapter, I'll break down each area in simple steps and leave you with actionable tasks to improve even the most dysfunctional team. One size doesn't fit all, we're not all the same, and over the next chapter you'll find out why and how to fix it.

Stuff like poorly handled enquiries are so avoidable and cost you thousands of pounds in profit each and every year. If I'm honest, I think most business owners have no idea how crucial it is. They have no system in place for handling enquiries and can't understand why they're not getting the £50,000 jobs coming through. It's not rocket science, and I'm going to break it down for you here.

Having ineffective or zero communication with your employees, then expecting them to buy into your ideas and philosophy and deliver world-class service is criminal. As you read every word of this chapter, think about your own business. Who answers the phone? You? How many calls do you miss? What do you say when you pick up?

We're not all the same, and I'm glad we're not

The more you know about someone, the more you get out of them. I'm a huge believer in knowing your team on a personal level. I never get confused by someone's personality and their attitude because their personality is a natural occurrence, but their attitude depends on what they think of me.

A business is essentially one big dysfunctional family. We've all got family members who are totally different yet have the same morals. We've also got relatives who are the same as we are but have different objectives. A business is identical in so many ways—apart from the way we view it ourselves.

From my own experience and working alongside many, many clients and their businesses, I wholeheartedly believe everyone should be the same at work, even if they're entirely different people outside of work. It's why we say things like, 'Don't bring your problems to work with you.' I mean, where else are people going to leave problems when they're at work? Ever tried dropping your problems off on a park bench while you go to work and then collecting them at the end of the day? You can't.

So, first of all, we have to accept everyone is different and everyone reacts differently to what appears to be the same situation. Unless we do, we won't get the commitment we're looking for. Often our expectation of commitment from someone we don't even know yet is scary. You expect new employees to start on day one with the same passion you have. No commitment to them, no commitment to you (paying someone a wage is not the same commitment as being employed).

Let me give you an example of why we're so different —just a simple story to show you we're not all the same. And why you may be trying to clone yourself.

There are four personality types. Here are two you'll be familiar with.

For years, my wife has complained I leave everything until the last minute. For the same amount of time, I've said my wife worries about things long before they need to be worried about. Let me explain how I figured this out and managed to improve every relationship I have, all by accepting my personality profile.

I booked a holiday in January 2016 and, as always, we paid a small deposit to secure the date. The nice lady at the travel agent gave us clear instructions, so we knew that the remainder of the deposit would come out at the end of February, and the balance would be due 12 weeks before the departure date. Pretty simple instructions, which I was perfectly comfortable with.

When we left the travel agent, my wife suggested we set up a savings account and deposit an exact weekly amount in there; then on the date the balance was due, we would be able to transfer it. I, however, had a different idea. Pay the remainder of the deposit on the day it was due and then the balance 12 weeks before the departure date, as the lady had instructed.

No point worrying about paying a bill until it's due. I know when it's due, and the money will be there, just like it always is. For the next few months, we had several disagreements about this. But why? It had to be paid 12 weeks before we went. Both of our plans had the same end result, yet we had far too many disagreements about how to achieve that result.

Where else does this happen in your business life and personal life? You find yourself having to fight to get things to work. You'll be sitting reading this and either seeing my point or my wife's point. Yes, she was right to save a bit each week, but so was I to pay it in one go on the day it was due.

They say a leopard never changes its spots, but people are not leopards, and if you can identify their personality type, you can help them change. That goes for you too. I said at the start of the book, I would give you your life back. This simple understanding will reduce your stress levels immensely because now you know you're not dealing with bad attitudes, just differences in personalities.

To get a clear-cut understanding of this system in detail, pick up a copy of *The Four Color Personalities For MLM: The Secret Language For Network Marketing* by Tom "Big Al" Schreiter. It's a cracking book that will have you laughing and face slapping as you recognise each and every person in your life from the story.

There really is no logic in emotion

I brought a Bentley Continental GT in a moment of emotion. My phone battery was dead, and I was in love with the Bentley. No going back. For the next ten days, while I waited to collect it, I had every conceivable emotion pouring into my daily thoughts. It's so expensive. I could buy a house for that.

For a year prior to getting the car, I had been teaching

sales systems to business owners like yourself. So, I completely understood the theory of selling on emotion vs logic. It's only when you're in the situation yourself you realise how powerfully it pulls you to a buying decision. All the way through the process you have one voice in your head saying this is not a good idea, and another voice saying, you deserve it.

When you're selling your prospect on the new garden, they're having these same conversations going on in their minds. Because a garden is a luxury item—it's something people want, not something they need. That's why you have to keep all communication focused on the emotion and not the logical brain (although as technicians, we can't help explaining the process of building a garden!)

When you communicate with prospects, it's important to keep them in the emotion of the purchase. They're buying future memories, fulfilling childhood dreams, not choosing paving slabs. No one has ever bought a garden from you; they've invested in an entertainment space for their family parties or a place to relax in retirement. When you sell the emotion, you increase the value. When you increase the value, you can increase the prices.

A good exercise for you to do is take out a notepad and on one side write down all the things you sell to clients and on the other side write down what they're going to do with what you sell them.

For example, you sell paving slabs, they get a BBQ space for family get-togethers. Or you sell fencing, they get security and privacy.

The real skill is to keep it simple.

Ordinary communication done extraordinarily well.

Give them a K.I.S.S.

 Everyone wants to go to heaven, but no one wants to die to get there.
~ Steve Jobs

What does that statement have to do with business, and running a landscaping team? Well, not a lot, but everything at the same time. Because everyone wants the dream, but they don't want to invest the money to achieve it. Or they're not always realistic about what they need to invest to achieve it.

The simpler your communication, the easier it is to get results. If I had to give a perfect example, it would be, 'If you want to know if someone is happy with the price you gave them—ask them.' Don't make a complicated business and relationships any more difficult for yourself. Get clear with people what you expect and what you're going to do, and then communicate it with them.

If you want something doing, tell your team you *want* it doing. If you want something doing, and you tell them you *need* it doing, you'll be chasing them for weeks to get it done. This applies to communicating with team members and potential clients. Team members want leadership from someone who has clear direction. Tell them what you want and when you want it.

Clients need to know when you'll be there and how they can get what it is you sell. What the next steps are, who they should be talking to, when they need to pay, and how they need to pay. You can't communicate enough with clients and team members—but don't make it complicated. Be consistent. How you do something is how you do everything.

Here's a good, simple tip for better communication that will save you from attending meetings where the other person doesn't show up. When you book a prospect in for an appointment, confirm it in writing. Don't assume they wrote down or remembered when you're coming to see them. I've made that mistake far too many times, and others just like it.

Mistakes are expensive unless you learn from them

As I've said before, if you're not making lots of mistakes, you're not moving fast enough. I love it when people make mistakes because it highlights a need to get better, upskill someone, or change a system.

If you're trying to prevent mistakes from happening, you'll be working too hard for too little in return. I say this from experience—no theory in this chapter!

Any mistake is solvable in business. As I just said, how you do something is how you do everything. So, it's not what happens, because what happens, happens to all of us; it's how we deal with what happens that defines us.

I've made more mistakes and had more customer complaints than you could imagine. Has it stopped my progress? At times, yes; but in the grand scheme of things, it's those mistakes that have helped me get to the point where my business runs without me needing to be there all day every day.

Sometimes the complaints and mistakes can be overwhelming, because like anything difficult, they tend to all come at once and beat the life out of you. Those feelings aren't unique to you.

You've probably had issues in the past you know you haven't dealt with in the best way. Maybe you never went back and fixed a problem. Or you walked away from something you really could have dealt with but didn't want to.

My biggest lesson around customer complaints happened before I started my business, but I fixed it when I set up my company.

I'll never forget the lesson I learned. I built a garden for a gentleman called Dr. Mike. The garden stepped in terraces, and I used reclaimed bricks to retain the soil.

When we finished the project, it looked fantastic. The client loved it, and we parted on very good client/contractor terms. He was happy to refer me to colleagues.

About 12 months later, there was a problem with the brickwork. The damp from the retained soil had got into the bricks and blown the face off them, and it looked awful.

I told Dr. Mike I would repair the wall and it would look great again. He said, "These things happen, as long as it's fixed, I'm ok with it," which suited me, and I left.

On the drive home, I had two overriding thoughts. Number one, I was a self-employed landscaper and had no money to correct this problem. Number two, I wondered if I could repoint it and buy myself another year to get the money to repair it properly.

I chose to repoint and buy myself more time because, financially, it was my only option. I completed the repair, and everyone was happy except me; I knew it was going to come back again next year.

As expected, almost 12 months later, Dr. Mike called with the same problem. Only this time, he wanted the wall rebuilding and wouldn't accept anything less. I promised to rebuild the wall.

For the next 12 months, I lived in dread of phone calls and having to keep putting him off. It was a horrible situation to be in, and I wanted desperately to do the repair; I just didn't have the money.

Fast forward a little bit, and I'd started my business after meeting my coach. About four or five months into building the company structure, he asked me, "What else is on your mind?"

"Dr. Mike's wall," I said.

We discussed what had happened, and I told him I needed to fix the issue because it didn't sit well with me. From an integrity perspective, I felt obliged to get the work redone.

I contacted Dr. Mike and apologised for going AWOL. He was surprised to hear from me. In fact, he said he'd given up on us doing the work, which made me feel good about contacting him.

Over the next week, we bought new bricks and rebuilt the whole wall. When we finished, it looked amazing, and I was happier than the client. I'd finally put this to bed.

I've never spoken to Dr. Mike since, and he never thanked me for the rebuild. Why should he? Quite frankly, I didn't mind, because I knew I had done the right thing.

This is just one of many mistakes I've either made or not been in a position to do anything about. But one way or another, I corrected them and learned valuable lessons from them.

If you have something like this hanging over you, take the bull by the horns, reach out to the client, and fix it. You'll feel liberated afterwards.

All of this could have been solved by having clarity about the task in hand. I wasn't clear about the problem I was fixing... and it was my responsibility to make sure I was.

You either have clarity, or you're creating drama

"It's bloody common sense!" How many times have you found yourself saying that? Yet common sense isn't that common. In fact, it's rare. Very rare, and if you have some common sense challenges, it might well be your own common sense you should be challenging. Nothing beats clarity, including common sense.

If you don't have clarity, you have drama. No one knows what's going on, who's in charge, where they should be. You name it, lack of clarity causes it. Usually simple stuff as well. 'Complete your timesheets each week and hand them in,' is a reasonably standard request and a simple one at that. But just this one request can cause lots of problems.

So, the straightforward way around it is to be crystal clear about expectations, which requires a whole lot of patience on your part. I work on this mantra: I'll say it and then say it again until you can say it.

Sometimes communication issues are down to the information given; other times, it's how people receive the information, which is why my system gets people's lives back—it eliminates drama.

You have to set every new team member, every new system, and every new project up to succeed, but most business owners set things up to fail. No notes. No past communications.

Every single task in your business should have a written process for it. Then everyone who uses it, or is affected by it, should be trained to understand it. Even then, you can use a simple coaching technique to make sure it all went in. I'll give it to you at the end of this section.

All your team members need job descriptions. Even landscapers. Just because they've done landscaping before doesn't mean they know what you expect. So, slow it down. Put every new member through a full induction. In a small business where you have all the systems in your head, you can get the new member to shadow you for the entirety of their first day. That investment will pay off for you.

I'm amazed at how many businesses I get invited to where they don't have written schedules for their teams to follow. Teams just get sent to the job site and told, "You have ten days to complete the job."

Or the boss goes out every morning to tell them what needs doing. This method is making an already tough job even tougher, for three reasons:

- You're training your team to rely on you every day
- You're creating a substantial extra workload for yourself by having to visit the sites every day
- You're giving your employees the excuse they need not to get the job done on time

Get everything you have in your head down on paper and run through it once with your team. From there, if you've hired the right people, they'll be able to follow the instructions.

The simple coaching question to know they understand what you have just told them is:

Ask them to repeat back what it is you just told them you wanted them to do.

Try it. You'll discover a lot of your communication issues are down to a simple moment you say something they hear differently. Specifically, you say something without checking they heard it correctly.

Any time you offer a solution to a problem, but you

haven't listened carefully enough to understand, you're in trouble.

Never offer a solution until you understand the problem

The next call you get could be your dream client with an unlimited budget; are you confident you'll win the job when you answer the call?

Firstly, you must answer the phone every time it calls, not reply after you've missed it. If you're answering your business's calls and missing some (or all) of them, get the phone answering outsourced immediately.

Nothing frustrates a potential customer with money burning a hole in their pocket like a business that doesn't answer the phone. It's unprofessional and unreliable.

A business that doesn't answer the phone when it rings is quite literally throwing money down the drain. The thought process of a prospect is; if I can't get hold of you when I'm giving you my business, imagine what it'll be like when you've had my business?

That first impression is so critical to positioning the business, and the whole sales process hinges on first impressions. So much so, I'd be confident of saying it costs you the exact amount of work you think you need to be successful.

I get people who say they want more leads, and when you call, they don't answer the phone. It's usually not the right enquiries and clients they need; the problem is servicing the ones they have properly.

The first interaction with your business is the one the prospect remembers most, which means an unanswered phone could be their first impression. Not something you want too much of.

If you treat answering the phone like a currency, you

won't be far from the truth, especially when you understand all your marketing KPIs (key performance indicators). Once you have the cost per enquiry stats, you get very hot on this.

The other thing to get your head around is that you can't win a client in the first seven seconds, but you can lose them in that time. Again, for fear of sounding like a broken record, if you don't answer the phone, you've more often than not lost them.

Not in all cases. You'll still get business when you ring back—not everyone is as unforgiving as I am. It's the number you lose from not answering the phone that's frightening. And avoidable.

You do have some options. You can hire an administrator or outsource the calls to a telemarketing team. Whichever way you go, remember to script your call answerer. Collect all the information, ask the right questions, and engage them with emotion.

Make sure you hear the question before you answer it.

Don't answer every question

If you give someone the answer to their question, they won't need to talk to you again, especially on social media. Always answer a question with another question. You want to fact-find, build a rapport, and get something back for giving away your knowledge. Like anything, it takes patience.

Here's an example.

Someone asks you for a price on a garden design. Even though you know the answer, and you feel they're interested in buying it, ask them for an email address where you can send the design.

Once you've collected an email address, you can

communicate much better than you can on Facebook Messenger. It feels more professional and certainly looks more professional.

Social media is so instant and doesn't give you much time to connect. An email with plenty of detail in it slows down the buyer, who gets the full information rather than just a price.

We both know there are cheaper prices if you want substandard products. But in most cases, you'll find the serious prospects want to communicate off social media when they're ready to move forward.

I completely love Facebook for advertising, and it's worked wonders for me, but only for lead generation. Once someone expresses an interest, it needs to go to the next level of sophistication; an email, a phone call, or a video call. Something more professional.

So, simple tip with this one. Answer questions with questions, and don't give any prices away without getting an email address or phone number in exchange.

Take a few minutes to think about what you've learned in this chapter. Often communication is accidental. There's no real strategy to it. The most successful businesses have clear expectations about communication and do it magically.

In case you have any doubts about what I'm saying here—it doesn't matter how good you are at landscaping if you're poor at communicating.

An award-winning landscaper will lose out to a complete novice landscaper if the novice communicates better.

Summary

First impressions last, and great communication comes down to one fundamental thing; that you understand yourself and the people you're communicating with. Be clear, be precise, and follow up on all communication.

We're not all alike; we respond differently to the same instructions. Some people are more logical, and some people are more emotional; it's balance we're looking for.

Keep things simple, learn quickly from mistakes, and get clarity about what you and others want. Until you do, you can't offer a good solution to an already difficult decision.

Lesson 5

Create scripts for all communication with prospects and customers.

When you're ready to understand the full power of scripts and structure for your sales processes, head over to www.barryrandall.co.uk/booklessons and watch my video: **why small business owners should have scripts in sales...**

6

THE PROBLEM WITH GOALS

How to Create a Business and Life You Love in Simple, Tiny Steps

 A goal is not always meant to be reached. It often serves simply as something to aim at.
~ **Bruce Lee**

What does it truly mean to get a good work/life balance?

I believe that before you get a work/life balance, you need to get a good work/work balance. By that, I mean getting a balance between reactive working and proactive working. Nothing changes if you stay IN your business. IN your business is the firefighting side of it—dealing with problems, handling everything that needs doing now.

The more you can plan out your weeks and succeed in sticking to your plans without being sucked into the quagmire of problems, the more chance you have of creating balance. Think about it for a second. It doesn't matter how good you are at business, landscaping, and people management; the problems come and keep coming.

In fact, on an average day, you'll have tens of problems to react to. You have to systematise the reactions, and then it's responsive. The key is to respond to issues, not react to them. Only once you have all your systems and people in place will you have the perfect work/work balance. Then you can start to work on the life part.

Some people will read this and say, "Just don't do the work." Not that simple in a growing business. If you leave it and take a day off, the problems get bigger; they don't disappear.

Start by listing all the things you would like to do this week, and at the end of each day, write down the things that stopped you from doing them.

You'll see a pattern in the urgent work, and then you can start to ask questions like; what's the system answer instead of the people one? Without the systems in place, it's easy to blame the people, but you can't be the system for everything or the solution to every problem.

Remember, nothing improves until you do. You have the ability to change the results, but you can't influence them by doing it all. The answer to your work/life balance lies in your work/work balance.

Take it slowly, break it down, and just make small improvements every day.

Do as I say, but not as I do.

If I do simple things consistently, I'll beat your flashes of genius every time. I know this as a fact.

"Just a few simple disciplines actioned every day will get you a fortune, but a few simple disciplines missed every day will cost you a fortune."

That's another quote I picked up from Jim Rohn. Such a powerful message and such a simple way to fix everything in our lives. However, doing it is way more difficult than saying it. I know how crucial this is to my life, especially around my health. I still needed to hire a coach to help me with my fitness and eating habits.

A lot of people are planning for retirement, but not many are planning their health to make sure they'll still be here. Stress kills, and we're all going to struggle to reach big numbers if we don't get the right support around us.

With consistency, you have to be ready to hand over repetitive tasks to assistants. As soon as it's too much to post content on social media every day and check on your sales results, you know you need help.

We're all expert advice-givers, and then we slip off into our undisciplined world to hope for the best. Your team notices you aren't being consistent. Your family notices you aren't being consistent. Everyone notices.

Once you let it slip, it starts to show up in other areas of your life. Like I said before, how we do something is how we do everything. Show up every day. The goal isn't to become a genius; the genius is to become consistent.

It's as simple as showing up every day, having done what you said you would when you said you would. If you get this nailed down, you'll be heading for success. Forget all the knowledge you could ever acquire… you need to be consistent. Start today, and you'll change your tomorrow. Fail to follow those disciplines, and you'll burn out.

You need balance. This was something I had the unfortunate pain of learning the hard way back in 2013 when I was burning the candle at both ends.

I was low on work and took on a contract for a commercial turf-laying company. This particular weekend I had two projects running—one in Ipswich and one in Somerset.

I left home at 4 am and drove to Ipswich. We had to complete the project on the day, so I worked right through, and we finished at about 6.15 pm. I signed off with the site agent and then set off for Somerset.

I planned to get to Somerset around 11.30 pm, get a

good seven hours of sleep, and then be up on the Saturday morning because the project needed to be finished by 4 pm Sunday.

All went to plan with the driving, but on the Saturday, I woke up feeling very tired and a little stressed. Not wanting to let down the company, I went to the site, and we did a good day of work until around 5.30 pm.

That evening we went for a few drinks in the hotel bar, and I was feeling wrecked. I thought, if I go to bed and get a few extra hours sleep, I'll be fine in the morning.

I'd been back in my room for about 20 minutes when I started feeling a sense of tightness around my chest area. I laid there and tried to ignore the feeling and force myself to sleep. It continued for an hour or so, and I sat up and thought, I need to ring for an ambulance. Not wanting to look like an idiot, I decided just to lie back and wait for it to pass.

Eventually, it did, but I learned a valuable lesson.

Number one, listen to your body. When it's time to slow down, do it. If you don't, nature will force your hand, and it could be fatal. You only get one body, and you need to be careful what you do with it.

Number two, I've been programmed from an early age not to ask for help because it's a sign of weakness. What if those chest pains had been a heart attack? I would have been too 'brave' to save myself.

How and when to do goal setting

> All our dreams will come true if we have the courage to pursue them.
> ~Walt Disney

A major factor in my recent success has been down to goal setting. I remember my coach, Alan, asking me for the first time what my goals were. I said, "To travel." Not backpacking around Australia, but luxury trips with my family.

I didn't believe it would all happen for me, but I started a list anyway:

- Dubai
- Las Vegas
- Florida
- Los Angeles
- Mexico
- New York

The list was extensive, and at the time I had zero money; just a drive to make stuff happen and a coach who knew how to guide me. So, I started setting goals and using things I thought were cheesy.

Vision boards. Written goals that I would read back each night. Planning step by step. Making a list. To me, this felt awkward until it all started to happen.

Of course, it can't happen by magic; you have to make it happen with hard work and persistence. The difference with having goals was that it made decisions easier.

Once I knew where I was going with my business, all the decision-making was easier. But that came from having personal goals. The only reason to have a business was to have a better life.

If I asked you right now to set some goals, you'd find it easy enough to write down those for your work life. That part's straightforward. Instead, start with your personal goals. Go inside out with it. What do you genuinely want to achieve from life, and how will your business help you do that? That's the question to ask yourself.

Nothing is impossible. Someone had to 'see' the MacBook I'm writing on before they could make it. Someone had to 'see' the house you live in before they could build it. It's not magic.

Take out a pen and paper and write down a list of things you would like to achieve in your lifetime. Then beside each one put 1, for a 1-year goal, 3, for a 3-year goal, and 5, for a 5-year goal.

You may initially think about what you can afford now, and that's understandable; but for just a few minutes while doing this, imagine money wasn't an obstacle, and you could have, do, or be anything.

Let your goals pull you in the direction you deserve to go. Then be consistent. Teach people what you know. Lead by example, because you need a clear set of goals and a clear path for progress.

Different strokes for different folks

There are four personality types, and you're just one of them. But you need the others.

I won't venture too deeply into this subject because the books that I learned from explain this in much more detail.

However, I wanted to give you an overview of what I learned and how it's impacted my whole business and life. The relationships I have with people and why we're different.

Especially in goal setting and achieving goals. This brings up the visual and verbal argument, but again both have a valid reason for working. Just depends on which you are.

I'm definitely more of a visual person. You can tell me

everything you want over the phone, but I still need to see it in writing before I can say yes. Doesn't matter about the value of the thing, I have to see it.

Your customers, employees, and suppliers all have different communication preferences. Some need a simple explanation over the phone, and others require a full brief and debrief.

It's your job to work out who needs what and make sure you deliver it the right way. The alternative is to create a system that handles all four personality types at the same time.

A prime example of this is booking holidays with a travel agent. They take a small deposit and tell you when the payments are due, with the balance typically payable 14 weeks before you fly.

My wife sees this as simply putting a small amount away each week, starting from now, so the money is ready when the payment falls due. I see it as I need the balance 14 weeks before we fly.

Does this cause friction? Yes, absolutely it does. But both approaches have the same result in the end. I have one way of handling business. My wife has another. Same result, different styles.

In simple terms, the four types are the driver, the influencer, the compiler, and the thinker. Every one of them has a different set of goals and different ways of reaching them. You can learn something from all of them, just like I did.

We're all different

We're all different. That's not bad, but it's not good either.

Let me explain:

Life is complex. Landscaping is complex. We're

complex. Clients are complex—my goodness they're complex!

To add to this whole mess, we have massive potential complications in delivering a project. Weather, suppliers, sickness, anxieties, other people's opinions.

You see how this becomes a muddle very quickly, for apparently no real reason? You probably also see how this is difficult to pin down to one key thing.

Some people are real planners; others just go in both feet first. Neither is wrong. They both have a massive part to play in your business (and your life). The bit we get wrong is knowing who plays which part.

Often our instinct is to go and hire someone who is 'quick.' Someone who can get the job done. But that whole concept is subjective. What is getting the job done, really? It's about quality.

Personally, I work at a ferocious pace. If I were on site, I would be laying the bulk of the paving—give me 75m2 paving, and I'll put it down for you in a day.

The problem with complexity is, if you give me the set-up of the paving, the first part, my pace is too quick for that. The set up requires a planner. A thinker.

Is that frustrating for me? Yeah, absolutely. Planners go at a snail's pace for me. I want to push them out of the way and let me get stuck in. Take over. Rush the job along.

It's a bit like the old hare and tortoise fable.

We're not all the same, and that's perfectly ok, as long as you recognise this early. Be aware of what you need, who you have in the team, and how each one adds value. Right bums on the right seats. Round pegs in round holes. Whichever analogy works best for you.

Think about your current team and yourself. Are you trying to be a hare when you're a tortoise? Play to strengths in yourself as well as your team.

Where are you asking a tortoise to be a hare?

Where are you asking a hare to be a tortoise?

You have to help everyone see the goal differently, and you need to accept the different personality types when you hire.

Everyone works better with schedules

Everything in your business should be running to a schedule. Everyone in the business should be running to a schedule. Most importantly, you should be running to a schedule.

If your teams rely on you to be there to let them know what to do next, you've got to get the schedule out of your head and on to a system. Paper or cloud-based. Make it visual, make sure everyone is aware of the schedules, and if they go off track, write out new schedules. Otherwise, it's pure carnage, and you're relying on people using common sense (which is woefully uncommon).

Here are a few suggestions for schedules:

Project tracking

Everyone who runs a project should be working from a written schedule. It doesn't need to be overly complicated, just a list of things that need doing on a certain day and when materials are due to arrive.

Project management

Everyone involved in a project should have a plan. When you'll be calling a customer, what day materials need ordering, when the invoice is due.

Business development

All members of the team involved in implementing new strategies should be following a written plan. This plan should be the subject of a weekly discussion until the project is complete.

Sales management

You should schedule in every member of your sales team (and yourself if you're selling), the client should know when you're coming, and you should be calling them prior to arriving.

The biggest one—which always gets overlooked—is time to work on your business or to relax and think. Not one person has ever mastered this (that I'm aware of).

If you set time aside to work ON your business, make follow-up sales calls, go through job applications, or write marketing copy, but something always comes up and takes the time away, you need to schedule yourself into your diary.

Book it out. Make space. Have the discipline to see it through. Make time for yourself in your busy life. If you don't schedule it and treat yourself in the same way you treat a client, you'll never get time to work ON your business.

Just go to your diary and put in, 'meeting with Barry[1].' Make it an immovable appointment. Set yourself up with an agenda and then don't let any outside distractions in.

Just some thinking time. A chance to make those calls. Time to finish the copy for your website. Some space to check your financials, call the accountant, or merely take some rest.

If you have no value for your own time, why should

anyone else? Being in service is great for customer service, but not great for personal service. You're the prize racehorse, so don't run every race.

Just make small sustainable improvements

What if I changed my thinking from 'this week' to 'this time in 25 years'? What would the potential be? Would it make it easier? Is it possible?

You see, the majority of people want to have everything, and they want everything NOW. Not always possible. In fact, almost impossible (although I don't often agree with the word impossible).

But think it through. If you improve your business by 1% each week, you'll be 52% better at the end of the year. Simple maths and much more realistic. It takes away the overwhelm of so much immediate change.

The most significant benefit of small changes is that you can measure how effective the change was. If you change 50 things at once, you won't know which part worked and which part didn't.

Change is needed. You know you need to change, which is why you're reading this book. What people don't realise is; change is more permanent if you do it effectively and intentionally.

Plan it. Think through the pros and cons. Then take concrete actions. But do it bit by bit. Start with the biggest challenge to your own time and then once you wrestle back the time, go for the profit.

Most importantly, take away the urgent pressure of doing things NOW, NOW, NOW.

And as most of us underestimate what we can achieve in a year, but overestimate what we can achieve in a week, it's logical to start thinking longer term.

Dan Sullivan created the concept of having a 25-year framework for your business. His approach was to break down the next 25 years into 100 quarters, then improve the business 1% each quarter.

Twenty-five years might seem like a long time to finish a business, but it really isn't because it'll be finished lots of times in those 25 years. By setting goals, such as having three teams and a manager, when you get to that point, you've finished it.

Then you go again, only this time you take it to the next level. So, focusing on 1% of the business each quarter is a really smart approach to sustained success.

It's leverage on leverage. Compounding the growth and the effectiveness of changes every quarter. Those changes compound your wealth as well as your business, reinforcing it against outside threats like recessions.

Imagine the first quarter you fixed your lack of time issue. The second quarter you got your pricing structure right. The third quarter you hired a manager to run the business. The fourth quarter you implemented your marketing systems.

You start next year with no time constraints, the business charging the best prices, a manager to look after the day-to-day work, and a constant supply of leads. Those things remain, as you add another 4% the next year. I'm not saying this is the correct model for every business, but the principle is to focus on getting each part right before moving on. Try breaking down the next year into four quarters. If you could improve one thing each quarter, what would it be?

Start with your biggest challenge and then only do that next thing next. Forget all the other things you could do; just do that one thing. I did mine by using a simple schedule to track my progress against my goals.

Summary

Goal setting comes naturally to some and feels alien to others. Again, that doesn't make it any less effective. Goals are meant to stretch us, to pull us out of our comfort zone; essentially give us a fantasy world.

Have a set of rules for yourself and the same set of rules for others. And pay close attention to your body; it knows when it's time to take a rest. Good work/life balance could save your life.

Just make small improvements so you can measure them and see them through to completion. Something as simple as a schedule could make all the difference when you're setting your goals and moving on them.

Lesson 6

Create a dream board.

When you're ready to start planning a better business and building a better life, head over to www.barryrandall.-co.uk/booklessons and watch the video: **the power of goal setting...**

---

1. Insert your name, not my name.

7

HOW TO BUILD BRILLIANT TEAMS

You Can't Do it All—So Build a Dream Team to Help You

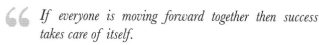 *If everyone is moving forward together then success takes care of itself.*
~ Henry Ford

My friend once sent me an email with the subject line, "You're not busy, you're lazy," which hit me right in the guilty face. The idea of 'busy' as a form of lazy, because we're not doing the things we need to do, hurt like hell.

Being busy is, in reality, a mindset, and not a very helpful one. It stops us from doing the things we should be free to do and enjoy. Life is passing us by on every busy day we get trapped in.

How many times do you bump into an old friend, and they ask you if you're busy?

Busy has become the new normal, or a badge of honour for people in business. A badge no one likes wearing, ironically. Most of us say it without even realising we're doing it. It's our go-to response, a bit like 'not bad' when people ask how things are.

When people say they're not bad, they're effectively saying they're usually bad, but today they're not. It's amazing how this affects us mentally. So, when people tell me they're busy, I either think they're not interested in a conversation (saying you're busy should make the other person leave you alone), or they're disorganised and don't have their priorities in order.

After all, you plan your own day. You set out your own week. So, if you're busy, it's by choice. Which is a bit of a rant, because it annoys me when people claim to be busy. I think it's a lazy comment.

I find there are a few things that typically make people busier than they should be:

- Poor pricing models
- Lack of systems
- Starting the week without a plan
- No overall vision
- Not delegating low-value tasks
- Excuses for poor performance

I don't want to go into detail on all these things, but I will cover the excuses for poor performance as I think it's the foundation of all the above. Business is already tough, as I've said a few times, so being busy can sometimes be the excuse we need to not be on top of our game. It also helps you to avoid the trickier side of managing your employees.

I sincerely believe we choose to be busy. In a world of hustle and bustle, where movement is often compared to productivity (which is totally wrong), it almost feels shameful not to be busy all the time. It's the biggest reason why thinking time is so infrequently used and undervalued by business owners.

Why would someone sit and just think when they can be moving around?

It's that mindset of needing to be busy to feel like you're making progress, which is so addictive. It prevents you from slowing down and working on higher-value work. That work requires time to think, and you can't do that when you're busy.

If you're busy and making a huge profit, then I'm ok if you dismiss this theory. But what I would say to people who are always busy is, what are you busy doing? My next-door neighbour's puppy is busy—really busy—but it's not achieving anything as such.

I suppose busy puppies are enjoying themselves, so that's something. But most people aren't busy and enjoying themselves; they're busy and miserable. So, give yourself permission to stop for 30 minutes a day. Treat yourself like you treat your customers. In fact, here's a tip for you:

Book yourself into your diary and treat it as if it were a customer appointment. Allow yourself to take some time to think. By stepping back and contemplating what it is that's causing your overwhelm, you get to make clearer decisions. Those decisions allowed me to relinquish control.

I was never in control of my business while I was trying to control all of it. I had to let go.

Control comes from letting go

"You'll know when you're a good manager... you will never be busy."

I first dismissed this as someone being cocky because they had a business that worked without them, but it makes sense now. If you're doing everything, who's doing what you should be? Who's running the business?

I know you're the best person to do the sales... I know

you're the best person to do the project… I also know you're the best person to do the aftercare.

Here's the thing.

I also know you've never given someone else the responsibility to find out if you are or not. You may have given them the task of doing the aftercare, but have you given them the responsibility? All of it? Including:

- Meeting the client
- Assessing the problem
- Costing the repairs
- Doing the repairs
- Getting feedback from the client

There's so much to each role, you'll never do them all effectively. I say that from experience. I've tried. Failed. Tried. Failed. So many times. The reason I kept repeating the cycle was down to me wanting to make sure every client got the best possible experience from us.

- I don't want bad reviews on social media
- I don't want problems getting paid
- I don't want to let the customer down

The problem was that while I was trying to prevent it from happening, it was happening more. You spend half your time trying to keep customers happy, and the other half upsetting them.

If you want complete control, you need to let go of every function in your business. Then you're left with the one role that only you can perform. You are your most important asset, but you're also your most expensive problem.

Holding on can do more damage than letting go. And

so what if you make mistakes? Aren't we all just learning? Even in defeat, we learn. We understand what we must do better to win.

From that thought process, I decided I would either win (job got done on time) or I would learn (what stopped the job getting done on time). Here's what I did.

The whole is bigger than the sum of all parts

It took a 10-hour flight to Atlanta, Georgia, and three intensive days in a coaching program called Money and You for me to learn it wasn't the individual people that made a business strong, it was the collective unit.

There really is no I in team.

The person delivering the coaching said, "The whole is greater than the sum of the parts," which particularly resonated with me. It explained why it wasn't as simple as doing a good job. It was what happened leading up to, during, and afterwards. The processes, the people, the experience, the different personalities… the whole circular nature of working as a team.

I came away from a programme that I'd attended to learn more about making lots of money, having learned more about myself, and how I viewed the world and the people within it.

If I look after the members of my team effectively, they'll look after the clients properly, and the clients will want to look after us in return. If that's true, I thought, I need to fix all of it. It wasn't just, find a great landscaper; it was looking at the whole picture and saying, what's missing?

If someone is a great landscaper, but they leave a mess behind them, is it better to keep nagging them about the mess or put someone in the team who likes cleaning up?

When I accept there isn't likely to be an abundance of people who can deliver a great job every time without any management, I can look at a different solution to the way I deliver my service.

When I do simple things like writing down the work schedule, I don't have to be present on every project to instruct people. Because even the best employees in the industry won't be able to read our minds.

That's why a system for the way you deliver your service is as, if not more, important than the person tasked with delivering it. When you're the only one who can deliver the project correctly or the whole plan is in your head, you'll never be happy with the people you've hired.

You need a system for the way you deliver your service, otherwise ONLY you can deliver it correctly. If it's in your head and therefore needs another you, you're screwed.

Clarity reduces drama. You can be onsite every day when it's one team. When it's two? You can't. Two jobs running means two teams. Two teams = two sales. Two sales = two jobs to organise, ahead of you and behind you.

One of anything is seriously destructive for your business. But one of you is even more damaging. It's these blind spots we have that prevent proper growth. That's what I see.

I see what you don't.

In your business.

In just one hour a week.

But before you start building a team, you need to know legally, and practically, how to hire and how to develop those people.

Hire people better than you

What do you honestly mean by, "I don't trust anyone to do the job properly?" I don't trust anyone 100%, but I trust them all enough to do their job. That's because I've managed to separate trust into different mental filing cabinets.

I see trust as something multifaceted. It's much more complex than someone letting you down. Do I trust YOU to take as much care of my car when you're driving it as I would if I were driving it? No, of course not. Why would you care as much as I do?

Do I trust you to do a good job when I'm paying you? Hell yes, because I have a system we would both follow. Same for me as it is for you. How can the results be different?

So, the real question isn't about trust; it's about who, what, and how. Who is going to do the job, what do I expect from you, and how are we going to get the job finished?

Once you're in alignment, trust becomes less of an issue. You can let go of the role and let someone else learn from their mistakes; release control and all the other things you know work for you. Your job is to be the leader; the people your business employs are responsible for its growth. You have to learn to separate trust in the grandiose sense, from allowing someone to mess up a little.

If you hire people who are more experienced than you are, you learn a little from them too. I appreciate how difficult that is because you have doubts about whether you have the knowledge and respect to manage them.

Like I said, you lead, they grow the business. You're presenting the opportunity from which they must take action and make it work.

I'll reference my client Michael again. Every time we hire new team members, I remind him it's the employees' responsibility to make it work. As long as they're sure of the expectations and have clear rules and policies, it's up to them.

Trust in the workplace comes from competence. If someone can do a good job, we trust them. If it's that simple, just hire people who are professionals in their field.

This is the same as not making mistakes. You have to put yourself out there in the marketplace to find out. Don't struggle through feeling like you've got to be the salesperson for your business, knowing you don't like selling to people and talking about money.

Bring someone in who does like it, so you can do the things you like doing. You wouldn't go and look for a job in sales if you didn't like selling. You wouldn't look twice at the advert. Why put yourself through it because you're the business owner?

You don't have to have all the answers. You don't have to be brilliant at everything. You have the opportunity someone else is desperately seeking. It's those individual relationships that allow you to build a formidable unit. If you look after your team as well as you look after your clients, you'll never lose good people.

That's why the whole is bigger than the sum of all parts.

When it all goes wrong

You're either winning or learning. No such thing as losing. The best business owners in the world get stuff wrong. If something can go wrong, it probably will; the mistake is not having a plan in place for when it does.

It's an intense world when you're in prevention

mindset. Preventing mistakes is the ultimate scarcity mindset. If you're not making mistakes, you're not progressing fast enough. Fail fast, I say.

Make a plan and attack it. Every step of your business journey is a learning curve, and the value in those lessons is worth more than any profit you can make on a single project. You can't unlearn anything, including mistakes. But most successful people learn more from mistakes—you never really analyse your business when it's working well.

For that one reason, making mistakes should be invited. Push yourself, push the boundaries, take chances. Especially with price increases and hiring staff. Business owners wait too long to make those decisions.

If something isn't going to work out, isn't it best to find out before you build a vast plan around it? Get started; you can get perfect later on. The longer you analyse something, the more you see the pitfalls.

It's not uncommon for me to have a success rate as low as 1 in 10 when I'm trialling new recruits for a trainee or landscaping role. Same for the clients using the system in our higher-level Black Diamond mentoring group.

I always use the 'What's the worst that can happen and if it happens, can I get around it?' question to make decisions. Sounds so simple, but often the best processes are.

What are you putting off because you can't get past thinking it could all go wrong? We all catastrophise things in our own minds. Talk about it. Share your feelings with someone. See if it's just you.

It is risky growing your business; it's also risky not growing it. Having a timid approach to expanding your business is much more harmful than the lessons you learn from mistakes.

A client once said, "You can always get the money

back, but you can't get the time back from running your business badly." I think that's as good an assessment as anyone could ever give. If you don't get it right, you learn the lessons from it. If you learn the lessons from it, you never get it wrong again.

Think about it. I can get it wrong, fix it, and move on to bigger and better things. Or I can keep thinking about all the things that could go wrong, never try it, and never know.

Whatever it is you're putting off for fear it might all go wrong, ask yourself MY question: If it goes wrong, can I get over it?

Then you can move on to the best part of business—hiring great people.

You don't need them to like you; you need them to respect you

Like all of us, Michael wanted to be liked. When he first became my client, one of his biggest concerns, as the business grew, was that the team should still like him.

But you know as well as I do that not everyone is going to like you. I told him, "They don't need to like you; they need to respect you." Two entirely different things. You're the boss; not everyone will like you—for a number of reasons. I'm sure you know what they are already.

The events with COVID-19 should tell you, sometimes you have to make tough decisions in the best interests of everyone, and individually that hurts. If they understand why you make those decisions and you include them in your business planning, they'll respect it more.

If they like you personally, then those tough decisions become emotional instead of process-driven. It's ok to show emotion, just make sure you have a good boss/employee relationship first.

People want to work for passionate owners. They want to feel inspired by someone who is a strong leader. So, absolutely you should build a relationship with your team, just build it on respect.

Respect comes from making significant decisions, giving people opportunities, and trusting them to make their own mistakes. It doesn't come from extra cash, gifts, and a pint down the pub.

Everything has its place, and all those things mean something to someone at some time. Just don't buy people's respect. Earn it. Don't ask someone to do something you wouldn't be prepared to do yourself.

By the way, you could start with a simple text message saying thank you to a member of your team. Not for a job well done, just to show your gratitude for them being with you. No big ideas here, just uncomplicated ones anyone (no matter how little time you have) could easily implement.

If you lead well, see potential in them, and provide opportunities, you'll become respected, and if you're fortunate, they'll like you too.

Legal and practical advice about hiring employees

I don't intend to make this book about HR, but there is some useful information I want to share with you. Remember, we're signing an emotional contract, so make sure you buy in if you want your employees to.

To me, there are seven things everyone should know before and about hiring great team members. These seven things will help you not mess this up; without them, it could be a disaster. I don't want that to put you off hiring people, because I know what it's like to take on team members and then find out what you should have had in place.

It causes a bit of panic. So, don't. Let this guide you through the ins and outs of hiring team members. If you want more insights, at the bottom of this chapter there's a link to an interview I did with a strategic HR expert.

I caught her off guard and made a point of challenging the whys and hows to make sure we're not all being made to do something that isn't wholly necessary. You'll love this:

1. An employment contract: This is to cover the basics, like working hours, salary or hourly pay, holiday entitlement, and any bonuses. You can get a contract from a good HR organisation for a small one-off fee.

2. A positional contract: The key success objectives of the role. Exactly what you've hired them to do for the company, and how they can succeed in the role. A little different to the employment contract because it's less legal and more directional.

3. A job description: This lists out everything they're going to be doing on a daily basis. If they're a landscaper, it'll be things like delivering landscaping projects on time and to a high standard. If they're an administrator, it might be to answer all inbound phone calls.

4. A set of KPIs: Key performance indicators are the primary statistics you measure someone against. For example, the number of days a project ran over target, quantity of good customer feedback, or value of work produced in a month.

5. Structured probationary reviews: How you do something is how you do everything, so start as you mean to go on. Make sure you do a one-

hour probationary review at the end of months 1-6. You can identify their concerns and address yours in these meetings to help make the probationary period a success.

6. A good training plan: You can't just hire someone and expect them to be a superstar. Everyone needs training. Everyone. Plus, employees want to know you value them, and one of the best ways to demonstrate that is to invest in their training and development. People don't want money; they want recognition.

7. A solid set of rules and policies: What time do you expect them to be at work each day? What happens if they're late? Who do they ask for holiday? What are the site rules? If you don't set this up at the beginning, it's an uphill battle later on.

That's a very brief description of what you need. At the end of the chapter there's a link to the interview I did that answers all the questions you might have about hiring people and getting it right.

I believe in you until you believe in yourself

I love giving opportunities to my team members. It's always a much bigger opportunity than they ever thought they would get, which builds on the emotional bank account.

It's also a great feeling to be able to give someone a chance. To have someone who believes in you—even when you don't believe in yourself—is so unbelievably powerful.

I remember my coach giving me some extra time to pay his fees when we were first working together. He told me he believed in me, he told me I would undoubtedly succeed, and he told me to believe in myself.

All these concepts were new to me, but I felt so good. I had this person who was successful in business, saying he believed in me. It made me more determined to show him I could live up to that belief.

This happens with your team too. I have five managers in my landscaping business, and each one of them has earned a promotion as the business has grown. I have never hired a manager. Ever.

All of them are extremely grateful for that. To be given a lot of responsibility. To be let into the inner circle and be trusted with the business's success is a huge feather in their cap for most people.

Especially for the ones who didn't ever think the opportunity would come. You're their mentor in many respects. You're helping them see the potential in themselves.

Maya Angelou said, "I've learned that people will forget what you said, people will forget what you did, but people will never forget how you made them feel."

Summary

I was racing around for 15 hours every day, like a hamster on a wheel. Wearing myself out but getting absolutely nowhere. I was in debt, and my wife was in tears at how bad our personal finances had become.

Everyone has a challenge with running a business— you're not alone. Just having the courage to step back and let go helps you manage the overwhelm much better.

Yes, there'll be mistakes, but so what? You have to trust people to do a great job because the whole is bigger than the sum of its parts. Just hire great people, believe in them, give them opportunities, and allow everyone, including yourself, to make mistakes.

Lesson 7

Hire a good HR consultant before you start taking on employees.

When you're ready to start taking on employees or need advice on how to fix your management and development processes, head over to www.barryrandall.co.uk/booklessons and watch the video: **everything you need to know before taking on employees...**

8

THE POWER OF COACHING

When You Hit a Plateau, This is How You Get Moving Again

 A coach is someone who can give correction without resentment.
~ John Wooden

I don't want to be told what to do in my own business. Who would! But that's not what coaching is all about. I want to remind you, I was £90k in debt, five months behind on two mortgages, and I was on the verge of losing it all. Without the intervention of my coach, I have no idea where I would be today.

Now I'm on the other side of the fence, I see it so clearly. With different personal circumstances, it's easy to see what was holding me back. Although, even with those insights, I won't be able to explain the true power of coaching; you have to get it.

I remember once I met a prospect who was in a panic and anxious for his business to become more sustainable. He'd got into financial difficulty and didn't see any way out.

A client of mine recommended this business owner

speak to me because I'd helped to grow my client's business, and it was now much more solid and financially secure in just three months of working together.

I had a call with the prospect, and the first thing he said was, "I don't want someone to come in and tell me what to do in my own business." Light bulb moment; I felt the same way.

The challenge was that someone telling him what to do with his own business was exactly what he needed. But I understood him because I'd been that person before. He needed someone to show him where the business was failing him.

Believe me, it wasn't a lack of effort. I don't know you, but I know you work damn hard and yet you're still struggling to get everything done. You're still struggling to make maximum profits or hire the best people.

Accountability, in a nutshell, is someone working alongside you to make sure you do the thing you know needs doing despite all the other noise going on inside your head. Not telling you what to do, just pointing out what you need to do, then making sure you get it done. Allowing you to show up every day, having done what you said you were going to do, when you said you were going to do it.

Those basic levels of accountability move the compass needle in your business, and instead of being blown in the direction of the wind, you start setting the sail.

We all want business-owner freedom and employee work, but it just doesn't turn out that way if you have a role in your business, like I do. I'm the part-time managing director. I know if I don't show up, the business doesn't function as well.

I started with a mountain of problems, and like you, I didn't want someone telling me what to do in my own business, but I needed help. I needed someone who could get the best out of me.

I needed a coach.

Just watch the ball onto the racquet

Why does Roger Federer have a coach?

Seriously, why would the greatest tennis player who ever played the game need a coach? If the coach is that good that he can make Federer better, why wasn't, or isn't, he a 20-time grand slam winner in his own right?

It's wonderfully simple.

Federer's coach isn't there to play tennis; he's there to see the things Federer can't see when he's playing tennis. Roger Federer's job on the court is to watch the ball on to the racquet. If he does that part well, the coach can focus on the other aspects of the game.

Let me translate this back to your landscaping business for a second because it'll mean more. In your business, you're doing the landscaping or organising the landscaping teams. Maybe selling the work.

Whatever it is you're doing; if you're conducting the day to day organising and running of the business, who's keeping an eye on the direction the business is going in?

If you have a coach—they do.

If you don't have a coach—nobody does.

That's the power of coaching. Having the eyes and ears of someone who's been where you are now, and achieved what you want to achieve, watching over you like a guardian angel.

I could go on and on about this subject, but I hope I have your attention.

Last thing to do.

Think of all the sports teams and individuals you

admire and do a Google search on them. If any of them are super successful and they don't have a coach (or two) email me, and I'll give you a refund on this book.

The power of coaching is incredible. Do you genuinely think Roger Federer, Manny Pacquiao, Cristiano Ronaldo, Ronnie O'Sullivan, or any other sports professional at the very pinnacle of their profession, did this alone?

They simply couldn't do it. They'd have too many blind spots, and wouldn't be able to see it from the right perspective to achieve outstanding performance. Simply because being IN your business doesn't allow you to work ON your business. The problems you think you're having in your business are never the real problem. That's what coaching clarifies for you.

But I'm like you; I didn't want to look stupid. So, I took my time before deciding.

I'll look an idiot if it doesn't work out

When I met my coach, Alan Brighton, for the first time, I did so in a café in the village where I live. Not somewhere I would frequent usually. I wanted to make sure no one saw me with him.

I can only describe it as being a bit embarrassed if I had to explain I was meeting a business coach. Just because I knew that the alpha male friends I had would say, "What do you need a coach for?"

But everything Alan said spoke to the real me. The person I thought I was supposed to be was cocooning the person inside who I wanted to be. That's very deep, but it should resonate.

I know my friends and family elders would say stop complaining and get on with it. They would encourage me with "All you need is enough to pay the bills and a few beers at the weekend." But I wanted more than that. I wanted bigger rewards.

Again, the fear of rejection was playing a big part in my decisions. If I hired a coach and he ran off with my money (seriously, I was that sceptical) I'd look a complete idiot... and it would probably crush me.

What if my friends and family find out I needed to hire a business coach—they'll think I'm incompetent! I'm supposed to be someone they look up to, and now this old (sorry coach) accountant-looking guy is telling me what to do.

Saying it now makes me laugh to myself, but I genuinely felt like I was a failure for asking for help. Six businesses later? So many lives changed. An extremely happy family. I'm the proudest person on the planet. It was the best decision I ever made to ask for help. Was I embarrassed? Yes, I was. The embarrassment was probably a stronger emotion than the excitement of what could happen.

Now I get to help people overcome the embarrassment and then go on to achieve great things. You see, all your family really wants is for you to be happy. But they don't know how stressed you are because you're protecting them.

Coaching helped me break free from those shackles. It helped me become a better father. It helped me become a better husband. Yeah, I've changed; I had to. But it's all for the better.

That's the power of coaching. Not just to change behaviour, but to change my identity.

The iceberg needs to melt

Your friends and family see the tip of the iceberg with you. They only see what you want them to see. The bigger feelings, emotions, and problems lie below the surface. To a degree, out of harm's way. But you can't suppress it forever; eventually, it takes you down, just like the Titanic. Beware of that as you progress through life.

What we see is your actions and the results of those actions. What we don't see is the beliefs, the skills, the mindset behind those results. When you get to work on the areas below the surface, you get bigger and better results.

You can only do this by changing the way you identify yourself. If you genuinely believe you can't achieve your life ambitions, you won't. No matter what you tell yourself, or however many times you talk about it.

You have to change your identity, and to do that, you have to change your environment. This is not a 'grab yourself a phoney passport and head to Rio' conversation… although… (only kidding).

What I'm talking about is getting amongst people who are heading in the direction you are. The people who want to share their problems with you. Where it's safe to do that and get the emotional support you need.

Look, coaching isn't therapy. Far from it. So, don't think it's all 'ra ra' and spirituality; however it does make you look deeper into yourself, admit what you're not great at; and also realise what it is you want from your life.

Change your environment to one where everyone wants to be successful, and you have to be successful to fit in. Stick with the environment where everyone wants to get by, and you only have to get by to fit in.

If that's not enough for you, then move. Get up and go. As Jim Rohn says, "If you're not happy where you are, move. You're not a tree."

It's not just the physical environment; it's the people around you too.

I'm ready to be successful

Just absorb all the gold in this section of the book. You'll be glad you did. This is another lesson to come from coaching. A powerful lesson.

There's a very real success equation that suggests you are the average of the five people you spend the most time with. If it's true (and I can vouch for it as being 100% true), then you only have to spend time with five successful people.

When I first learned of this, I panicked and thought it meant dumping my friends… it didn't mean that at all. It meant being around people in your work life who are more successful than you.

Think about it, if you spent an hour or two with Richard Branson, do you think you would learn some stuff about business that would easily make you more money? Of course.

That's what coaching does for you. It puts you with other people who are succeeding, and then you succeed. You take that home and start to share it with your friends and family, and hey presto!

Likewise, if you spend time with five people who are always moaning about life, about how unfair their circumstances are, who spend every penny they make each week… it isn't rocket science.

Take 30 minutes tonight and write down a list of the five people you spend the most time with. Then, beside each one, list the things you both have in common. What is the common conversation you have?

Is it negative? Do you moan about the weather together? Do you complain about staff together? Or is it a joyous and positive conversation about how successful you are and want to be?

Conversations like that bring us together and stop us being lonely.

It's lonely at the top

Being a business owner is lonely. Especially when you're having a tough time of it. Who do you reach out to when you're struggling? Just a single conversation with the right person saves you so much heartache and prevents lots of mistakes.

It's never so simple for us business owners, though. It's genuinely lonely at times. The thing is, we need to be in isolation a lot to get the key things in our business done; yet isolation is painful.

So, there are two options. One is isolating yourself and getting work done that's strategic and requires considered thinking. Another is isolating yourself as a way to cope with problems.

I'm not here to say it's easy; if it were, you'd already be doing it, and I wouldn't need to support you or teach you anything. Never struggle in silence. Having emotional support, having someone to chew the fat with, is not only priceless but also an absolute necessity.

There's a lot going on in the media about mental health and campaigns around "It's ok not to be ok." Well, running a small business is damaging to your mental health. The stress levels, the feeling of helplessness, the sense of shame and embarrassment are authentic, which is what makes our Black Diamond mentoring groups so special.

As one of our mentees, David, said:

 I knew things needed to change. Just as I did, I saw Barry speak at an event in Leeds, and I knew straight away this was a guy I wanted to work with. In fact, the story he was telling was so similar to mine it was scary.

I went to a couple of Barry's one-day workshops, and then in January 2020 I bit the bullet and joined his Landscaper's Success Club Black Diamond group. Finally, I had someone who understood my problems. Someone who had been in the same trenches as me.

Using Barry's teachings has rapidly grown my business, in what could have been a very difficult year. Commercially I have more than doubled the size of my business—in less than a year! That's turnover AND profit. To cap it all, I have just booked my dream trip to see the British Lions tour South Africa in 2021, which I mark as a real benchmark of success.

Never go through it alone because there's no need. Just a bit of support from people who are going through the same thing or have been through the same thing is very rewarding.

When you're ready to give up going it alone and want to take your business to the pinnacle of the industry, hire a coach. If you're ready now, come and talk to me about the Black Diamonds. I'll share more in a moment.

Men think they must be the rock and foundation of the world (I know—it nearly cost me everything), not just in our families. This socialistic pressure is bullshit; the most successful males in business have NEVER done it alone.

Running a small business is one of the hardest gigs on the circuit, and the strongest person in my business is my wife. I make no secret of that.

Without her support, I'd still be pretending I was tough enough not to seek help. It needs to stop. Don't suffer in silence; reach out and let us support you.

Summary

Coaching gives you options. Choices. Accountability. It isn't someone telling you what to do. It's someone seeing things you can't. Just like the world's greatest sports people do.

If your focus is on running your business, who's growing it? If you're growing it, who's running it? Without this focus and a clear set of numbers driving your business, it's all a bit accidental.

Everyone, including me, thought I was going to look like a complete idiot if the money I invested in a business coach didn't work out. I'd have been embarrassed, but now I ask why? It's no different to pricing up a landscaping job and getting it a little bit wrong. But because of the self-imposed belief I should know the answers already, it felt so much bigger.

Hiring a coach isn't admitting failure; it's assuming control. We're only good at so much, then we need someone to help us with the things we're not so good at. When you're ready to be successful, you use that knowledge to grow.

It's a lonely gig being a business owner, and if you allow yourself to slip into a mindset of rowing your own canoe, you'll quickly be rowing towards a waterfall. The results are catastrophic. Turn around, head back, and take someone with you for moral support.

When you're ready to stop going it alone and get the help you need, follow the next steps at the end of this book.

Lesson 8

Never take advice from someone who hasn't been where you are now.

When you're ready to hear what business owners, just like you, have to say about working with me, take yourself here: www.barryrandall.co.uk/booklessons and watch the video: **why coaching works from the people who know...**

I'm proud of every one of these success stories.

9

CONCLUSION: BREAK THE MOULD

Everything You Need to Make an Informed Decision

 Do you want to know who you are? Don't ask. Act!
Action will delineate and define you.
~ Thomas Jefferson

Here's what this is all about.

The system fails people like you and me. The system is designed to make rich white men richer. They don't want you and I to know how to get out of the traps we're set—but I broke the mould. I broke the rules, busted out, and you can do it too.

Game one is over. It's time to enter game two. Only this time, with a whole new set of weapons. Eight chapters ago, you were at your wit's end, with nowhere to turn and staring down the barrel of a gun.

You dared to change, and that's the first and by far the biggest step to take.

You know as well as I do that without the right tools, even the simplest job is harder work than it needs to be. But just reading this book is not enough. You won't see real change until you take action. Until you push past those fears. Until you stop taking advice from people who haven't experienced your struggles and start getting to know who you are.

Before anything around us changes, we have to change our inner game. Having a great mindset is the sharpest tool in any business owner's toolbox.

Being £90,000 in debt with no visible way out was scary, but it's not even close to how scary it is to think I didn't know this advice existed. How scary to think I could have gone my whole life and never found out.

You don't have to be embarrassed about being a less-than-perfect business owner. I certainly wasn't perfect. You have the skills you need to succeed! Being a great tradesman is the foundation for a great business; all you need are the tools to take your business to the next level.

I started where you are now. I was terrified of going VAT registered. I was horrified at the prospect of HR. I was appalling at accounting. So, I gave all those things up. Not the VAT, HR, and accounting. I mean, I gave up the fear and anxieties.

And it was so simple to do. I accepted my weaknesses, brought people into my circle, and trusted them to take care of the things I wasn't good at—despite all the people telling me I was wrong to do it (who, by the way, are in the exact place they were eight years ago when I decided enough was enough).

My journey started with one book, just like this one, and I never looked back. I could have stopped reading and gone back to what felt comfortable. But like I said before, you can't unlearn something, and the lessons in the book started me down the path to success—so I kept going.

I wasn't the smartest person in the room; I struggled with spelling and numbers, but I rolled my sleeves up and built a reputation for getting stuff done. I made up in effort what I lacked in business knowledge—and that's something any landscaper can do.

Don't settle for anything less than you deserve. Stride out of your comfort zone and accept we're not perfect; none of us are. It's better to try and make mistakes than not try at all. Remember, we all fear failure. Those feelings never leave us, so let them drive you on. Just because someone is doing better than you on the outside, doesn't mean they're not suffering like you are on the inside. We all want a little more.

You don't need motivation. Motivation is a myth. All you need is the courage and confidence and commitment to give it a go—accept nothing less for you and your loved ones.

Do the work, and all your old money worries will disappear to be replaced by a new feeling of control around finances. You'll discover that it's not about what we get. It's what we *do* with what we get that matters. What you believe about money isn't true. It's not the root of all evil. It's also not only for rich people. You're rich already; just look at the people around you who love you.

Look for others to help, support, and drive you on. They need opportunity as much as you do. There are great people in the world who would absolutely want to work for and with you in your company. You have to believe that. But that takes trust; it takes self-care; it takes attention to detail.

Success doesn't happen overnight, so put one foot in front of the other and keep moving forward. Work at the relationships. I tell everyone who will listen (lots don't) if you don't love landscaping, it's the hardest job in the world. Business is already tough enough without feeling like you have to know everything, control everything, and take this thing on yourself all the time. People want to help, I want to help, your friends and family want to help. But you have to let us.

And, so what if it goes wrong from time to time, isn't that part of life? I remember teaching my children to ride their bikes. Do you think I gave up on them the first time they fell off? No, of course, I didn't, and neither would you.

Business is the same, you'll try things that don't work, and your team will question your decisions. At times you'll think they don't like you, but they don't need to like you, they need to respect you. Respect comes from great leadership. Great leadership is the bravery to keep pushing on despite the pain.

Remember this: no one will remember the attempts you make but don't succeed at, except you. No one will ever know how lonely it feels to be a small business owner. No one will be able to help you grow unless you let them see the real you.

Believe in yourself and get great people around who know their field. Then you don't have to be afraid of anything. It's not as scary to enter the world of employment law and VAT as you may think. Most HR consultants and accountants are worth their weight in gold. Several times over.

My client Matt says, "Barry is 100% on the journey with me, I believe he cares about the results." I say, don't take advice from someone who won't be around when the results come in.

All of this is about choices… just taking the next step. This book isn't written to sell you anything, it's written to sell you on the idea of what's possible. Remember my story: I started behind. I started £90,000 in debt and I made the breakthrough, and I believe you can too.

Let me tell you this story to show you what I mean. In

the years leading up to meeting my business coach, I worked alongside my brother Jeff doing landscaping. We were both sole traders. Each year we would both try desperately to keep each of our self-employed entities under the VAT threshold. So much so, we would sometimes turn down work or lose work for being too cheap.

The truth is, I was afraid of losing work if I increased my prices to add the VAT, and so was Jeff. We struggled along like this for a year or two before we set up a "proper" business. We both believed VAT to be a swamp not worth swimming in. It looked so confusing.

Then recently, I saw a conversation on a Facebook group for landscapers. It was familiar to me. It went like this.

"I want two bits of advice. 1. I have a landscaping job for a new build and the client says it's zero-rated VAT. What should I do? 2. I'm close to the VAT threshold with my business. What should I do?"

The answers this person received were scary, to say the least. There was a lot of advice being dished out by people who clearly had very little experience with either of these scenarios, and who had only ever taken advice from little Jonny down the pub.

The bad advice included:

- Tell them to pay by cash.
- Run a mile and tell them to get some other mug to do it.
- Don't go VAT registered the tax man will close you down.

Now, this story might make you chuckle, but this is the kind of advice being dished out on Facebook groups to people who desperately need help with their businesses. This advice is scary, dangerous, and sometimes illegal. Anyone unwittingly taking this advice is putting their business and lifestyle in danger.

People's livelihoods matter to me. The landscaping industry needs more professionalism, honesty, and informed, expert advice. All these things come in abundance with me.

On the day my world came crumbling down at the Citizens Advice Bureau, I needed to hear the truth more than I needed anything else in the world. Those words of honesty helped mend something inside of me that I was avoiding fixing.

Do you want to face the truth?

Do you want to know how to get out of the rut you're stuck in?

Do you want to stop repeating the same mistakes over and over again?

Then make the choice. Take the next step. Choose the right next path for you.

Ultimately, the buck stops with you. You have to own everything in your life. Where you are right now is down to you. Where you end up is down to you.

No more kidding yourself. Who do you want to be? What clients do you want to serve? When will you decide? All those unanswered questions holding you back: just answer them. And then do the next thing next.

Lesson 9

Follow the next steps in this book and watch your business transform under your feet...

NEXT STEPS

> You don't need to take all of the steps at once.
> Just take the next step next.
> ~ Me

I write books so you can see first-hand that it's possible to take your small landscaping business and become a bigger, more professional organisation.

Your ambition might be to win a handful of awards, or build a garden for a local charity, or maybe the lofty ambition of winning gold at RHS Chelsea. Doesn't matter.

If you've got this far, you need to know what's next, so here's a handful of helpful resources you can use to start your business down the road to future successes.

First, remember to take each small step at the end of each chapter. You can find all the extra resources here:

www.barryrandall.co.uk/booklessons

Next, join the Landscaper's Success Club Facebook group here:

www.facebook.com/groups/LandscapersSuccessClub

It's full of people who are intrigued about how landscaping businesses grow, and some who just want to post pictures of their latest garden. Others have read my first book: *Time, Team and Money*, attended my events, and taken my courses or private mentoring.

The Landscaper's Unlimited Success Report

If you're ready to go it alone with the most valuable guidance you can find, start small with this unique 16-20 page printed monthly report packed full of golden nuggets. It gets delivered to your home or office every month like clockwork. It's a unique publication filled with the most cutting edge, straight-to-the-point wisdom for savvy business owners.

It's the only publication written specifically to help landscape business owners with small business owner problems. Think of the *Landscaper's Unlimited Success Report* as a monthly workshop… combined with a good dose of reality. It focuses on the BIG 4 things for unlimited success: Advertising, Marketing, Business, and Mindset.

It covers:

- Pricing strategies and how pricing done correctly will ensure you charge what you want, not what your customer dictates.
- Before and after advertising and sales copy examples, so you see what to do and what not to do with your marketing budget.
- Case studies and real-life examples from members and clients for you to learn from and take action on in your own business.
- Special guest articles because I do not profess to know it all and don't pretend to, so there are guest slots from people in HR, accounting and such like.

There's also access to the USR Facebook group with Monday motivational videos, bonus training videos, and some 1-2-1 mentoring time.

When you're ready to take this step join us here:

www.landscaperssuccessclub.com/unlimited-success-report

The Landscaper's Black Diamond Mentoring Programme

If you're ready to get serious with a bigger step, take advantage of our premier offering for landscapers: The Black Diamond Group Mentoring Programme. You get access to the *Landscaper's Unlimited Success Report* delivered to your door every month, plus:

- **Sales Copy Critiques** from a titan of the copywriting world: Trevor "ToeCracker" Crook.
- **A Hot Seat:** 45 minutes of intense mentoring to identify the biggest obstacle in your business.
- **Member Discounts** on all future products released under the Landscaper's Success Club umbrella.
- **Mentoring Credits:** Each month of your membership you'll earn mentoring credits for you to use when you need them most.
- **Bonuses from Experts**: From time to time, we call in professionals in the world of accounting, sales, HR, and suchlike to add even more value.
- **A Business Health Check:** In the first four weeks we'll send you a business health check for you to gauge where your business is right now.

- **Judgement Day:** You get instant access to Trevor "ToeCracker" Crook's Judgement Day marketing and advertising audios and transcripts.
- **Inner Circle:** You get access to our diaries— the exact people who have helped us grow our businesses and develop our skill sets.

You name it, you get it.

When you're ready to join the top tier group mentoring programme and lift your business to the next level, visit:

www.landscaperssuccessclub.com/discover

About the Author

 No one cares how much you know, until they know how much you care.
~ Theodore Roosevelt

My earliest memory of business was going around knocking on doors and asking neighbours if they would like their grass cutting. I was about 12 years old. So, of course, I had a bunch of friends with me.

Thankfully for me, the neighbours were happy to pay cheap child labour, and I learned some valuable lessons about turning up on time and charging properly in those early years.

I started out brightly at secondary school but really struggled academically in the last few years. I really didn't enjoy classroom learning, and my early adventures cutting the neighbours' lawns started me down the path to becoming a landscape gardener.

I left school at 15 and went straight into full-time work. I worked all week and weekends too, just to make as much money as I could. I wasn't shy of hard graft. I got that from my family.

I grew up on a council estate called Northfields in Leicester. I was lucky enough to be brought up in an awesome, close, life-loving, working-class family. The estate I grew up on gave me the ethic and attitude to face any challenge. I'm extremely proud of where I come from.

Over those first years after I left school, I dabbled with

different jobs: export packing, shoemaker, roofing; you name it, I tried it. But somehow it always led back to landscaping.

I've been a landscaper on and off for 28 years. I'm very hands-on and practical. I've won multiple awards from BALI (British Association of Landscape Industries) national and principal to Marshall's regional and national awards. But a landscaper is not all I am.

My life took many twists and turns along the way. Marie and I had our first daughter when I was only 19 years old, and I found myself having to work all the hours I could to support a young family. The pressure wasn't always easy to deal with (as you'll discover in the book).

But it was worth it.

I'm a huge family man. I have an incredible wife— Marie—and two wonderful children: Lorelle and Lexie, plus a cute-as-buttons grandson Chayse. I love Christmas, which is the ultimate family time… I'm a bit of a kid at Christmas. I love all the cheesy songs. I make a massive effort. I eat way more than I ever should do at Christmas. And I owe that all to my amazing Mum who taught me the value of family and I love her dearly for it.

I was once asked by a client if I had any hobbies: I do. Spending time with my family. I enjoy it as much as you enjoy your hobbies.

While you're still trying to get your head around how someone who looks so young could have a grandson, I'll tell you a little about my life, taking hard knocks, and never giving up.

Let me start with the best question you could ever know the answer to. It's the first question I ask someone in an interview, and it always gets the most ridiculous answers.

"Tell me a bit about yourself… what makes you authentically *you*?"

When they hear this question, most people ramble through a list of past work experience and never really tell me anything about who they are, or what makes them unique.

We're all unique. There's only one of you, and there's definitely only one of me.

I really want to give you a peek under the bonnet of me and share a little slice of my life.

I dreamt of being a professional footballer, but when it became obvious I had two left feet and was better with a pint than a football, I tried my hand at being a rock star. To be fair, that worked out for a while; for seven years, I was a touring musician playing badly paid, badly attended gigs in the UK and Ireland. I loved the buzz and uncertainty of the music industry, constantly trying to sell myself to an audience. But it wasn't to be, and I eventually found myself in the unforgiving world of artist management and ended up co-producing music that featured on Radio 1.

I also booked bands for a festival main stage, held meetings with lots of record labels, and went to a whole host of glitzy music industry events. I still have many friends in the business today.

I'm sharing this because although I had no tangible success, I learned a lot of incredibly valuable lessons, which helped me develop my own management and negotiation styles in my businesses today. Working with ungrateful musicians who had unrealistic expectations makes dealing with clients and their low budgets a breeze.

What I learned enabled me to build a business that allows me to do one of my absolute favourite things: Travel.

I love travelling. I've been to so many places in the world, and I have so many places still to visit. My favourite three places—for lots of reasons—are Olu Deniz in Turkey, La Cala in Spain, and Dubai… closely followed by Las Vegas. Every year, I host a luxury retreat with my business partner and buddy Trevor "ToeCracker" Crook in a beautiful location. I'm lucky. And I have designed my life and business to enable me to do this.

I own the car I always wanted. I own a house I'm proud of. I live a life I'm excited by. And I make my family proud. What more could any person ever want from life?

I know the answer to that question.

I want to see others achieve the same thing. I push myself and my clients and employees and colleagues hard to get results because I take enormous pride in seeing a member of my team, a client, or business partner succeed in life. It's a huge passion of mine.

I own or part-own six different companies, all of which I put my heart and soul into. Every single person in those businesses has my full support, my full commitment, and will 100% achieve what they want from life.

But it wasn't always like that. It hasn't been easy. Nothing worth having ever is. For example, when I met my business coach for the first time, he asked me for an Excel spreadsheet, and I had no idea what that was.

That was eight years ago, when I had no idea what Microsoft was. That one embarrassing moment gave me the kick up the backside I needed to discover the secrets to marketing and growing a business successfully.

I could go on, but I'm sure in time we'll get to know each other better, and I'll be able to share all of what I know with you on your journey. One day, I'll be reading your "About the Author" page and be delighted I could help you in some way.

I know how important I am now. I know how important you are too. I want you to know you can make a difference, you are capable of amazing things, and with the help of this book, you'll find what you're looking for.

facebook.com/BarryRandallOfficial

instagram.com/barryrandallsinnercircle

linkedin.com/in/barry-randall

Bibliography
BOOKS MENTIONED OR RECOMMENDED

Atomic Habits by James Clear

Eat that Frog! Get More Of The Important Things Done Today by Brian Tracy

Ego is the Enemy by Ryan Holiday

Fish! A proven way to boost morale and improve results by Stephen C. Lundin

Grinding it Out: The Making of McDonald's by Ray Kroc

Happy Money: The Japanese Art of Making Peace with Your Money by Ken Honda

How to Be Brilliant: Change your ways in 90 days! by Michael Heppell

I'm Ok—You're Ok by Thomas A Harris, MD

Legacy: 15 Lessons in Leadership by James Kerr

Magnetic Marketing: How to Attract a Flood of New Customers That Pay, Stay, and Refer by Dan Kennedy

Polar Bear Pirates by Adrian Webster

Profit First by Mike Michalowicz

Radical Candor: How to Get What You Want by Saying What You Mean by Kim Scott

Scientific Advertising by Claude C. Hopkins

Shoe Dog: A Memoir by the Creator of NIKE by Phil Knight

Take Charge of Your Life by Jim Rohn

Tested Advertising Methods by John Caples

The Big Leap: Conquer Your Hidden Fear and Take Life to the Next Level by Gay Hendricks

The Chimp Paradox: The Mind Management Programme to Help You Achieve Success, Confidence and Happiness by Professor Steve Peters

The Day That Turns Your Life Around by Jim Rohn

The E-Myth by Michael Gerber

The Energy Bus: 10 Rules to Fuel Your Life, Work, and Team with Positive Energy by Jon Gordon

The Entrepreneur's Guide to Getting Your Shit Together Volume Two by John Carlton

The Four Color Personalities For MLM: The Secret Language For Network Marketing by Tom' Big Al' Schreiter

The Fred Factor: Every Person's Guide to Making the Ordinary Extraordinary! by Mark Sanborn

The Goal: A Process of Ongoing Improvement by Eliyahu M. Goldratt

The Go-Giver: A Little Story About a Powerful Business Idea by Bob Burg

The Positive Dog: A Story About the Power of Positivity by Jon Gordon

The Power of Habit: Why We Do What We Do, and How to Change by Charles Duhigg

Think and Grow Rich by Napoleon Hill

Triggers by Marshall Goldsmith

Unsexy Business by Jamie Waller

What Got You Here Won't Get You There by Marshall Goldsmith

Who Moved My Cheese by Dr. Spencer Johnson

Wink and Grow Rich by Roger Hamilton
Write to Sell: The Ultimate Guide to Copywriting by Andy Maslen

Also by Barry Randall

Time, Team, & Money

If you've enjoyed this book (or even if you haven't) will you write me a review on Amazon please?

Reviews mean a lot to authors and they help other people just like you find our books.

You can leave your review by visiting Amazon and typing "Do The Next Thing Next" into the Amazon search bar.

Printed in Great Britain
by Amazon